CW01391068

"For anyone trying to implement transformative change in their organization, this is a complete must-have. It's a remarkably waffle-free book that shows how to put theory into practice in the most practical of ways – with real-world examples of where it's worked and where it hasn't. It's genuinely a breath of fresh air and an invaluable read for anyone interested in using digital principles and tools to transform their organization."
Tom Lillywhite, Director of Digital Transformation, UK Labour Party

"Refreshingly free of waffle and ego, this is an incredibly valuable guide – in fact almost a recipe – for launching and landing meaningful digital and business transformation. Every page shares precision insights and immediately actionable suggestions with a simplicity and clarity that only comes from many years of walking the walk. As useful for someone starting their digital transformation journey as one despairing about their progress to date!"
Pete Herlihy, Lead Product Manager, UK Government Digital Service

"This is a great book that will be of huge help to those involved in digitally enabled transformation. It is intensely practical, with many good case studies, but also very readable. The book is aimed squarely at those responsible for initiating and leading the change rather than technical experts. From me it comes strongly recommended. I wish it had been written a long time ago."
Lord Kerslake, former Head of the UK Civil Service

"Digitalization will have a major impact on the way services are provided and how business is conducted. Digital transformation can seem like a daunting challenge to any business leader and it is essential that we all build our understanding and knowledge as these major changes take place. This excellent practical guide will help you achieve this and de-risk your transformation programme. The guide gives you the tools and advice that you will need to succeed as well as being a valuable resource for those leading any digital change process."
Ian Carruthers, Chancellor of the University of the West of England and former NHS Chief Executive

"Organizations globally are spending billions on digital transformation right now; for many, it is one of their very largest investment areas. But it is easy to waste money on technology, consulting and internal costs because organizations and leaders don't know what they are really trying to do, or how to achieve their goals. *The Practical Guide to Digital Transformation* is truly practical, with great examples, case studies and tips that will be of value to anyone tasked with delivery. I particularly liked the 'what you might say in your next meeting' list at the end of each chapter. This book is destined to become a well-used friend to many senior managers, consultants and business students.
Peter Smith, procurement expert and author of *Bad Buying*

"Organizations are more aware than ever of the need to transform themselves for the digital age. But many, perhaps most, still struggle. *The Practical Guide to Digital Transformation* is the ideal companion for any company serious about adaptation. Written by a leading digital transformation expert, it provides the ideas and vocabulary to bring about change, illuminated by incisive case studies. It is written in user-friendly language, guiding the reader through the 'whys' and 'hows' of making change happen. This outstanding guide is essential reading for decision-makers, digital leaders, and practitioners seeking to ensure that their organizations thrive now and in the future."
Tanya Filer, Digital State Project Lead, Bennett Institute for Public Policy, University of Cambridge, and founder of StateUp

"A really excellent step-by-step primer to help your organization get the very best from digital technology. It is clear but not dumbed down. It will expand the thinking of new and experienced digital leaders alike, and gives concrete, actionable ways of bringing your organization with you."
Phil Buckley, Prix Jeunesse and BIMA award-winning digital product manager

"This book provides a unique, pragmatic, real-world guide to digital transformation. Each chapter unlocks different aspects, viewpoints and the considerations needed to embed change in a multitude of environments. The book is pitched to all audiences, providing the tools needed for anyone interested or actively involved in digital transformation. Antonio has managed to pack the learning from his many years as a consultant into this wonderful book."
Gary McAllister, Chief Technology Officer for NHS London and author of *An Introduction to Digital Healthcare in the NHS*

The Practical Guide to Digital Transformation

Quickly master the essentials with tips, case studies and actionable advice

Antonio Weiss

KoganPage

First published in Great Britain and the United States in 2022 by Kogan Page Limited

2nd Floor, 45 Gee Street
London
EC1V 3RS
United Kingdom
www.koganpage.com

8 W 38th Street, Suite 902
New York, NY 10018
USA

4737/23 Ansari Road
Daryaganj
New Delhi 110002
India

Kogan Page books are printed on paper from sustainable forests.

ISBNs

Hardback   978 1 3986 0367 7
Paperback   978 1 3986 0365 3
Ebook   978 1 3986 0366 0

British Library Cataloguing-in-Publication Data

A CIP record for this book is available from the British Library.

Library of Congress Cataloging-in-Publication Data

[****]

Typeset by Integra Software Services, Pondicherry
Print production managed by Jellyfish
Printed and bound by CPI Group (UK) Ltd, Croydon CR0 4YY

CONTENTS

PART THREE
Doing digital 71

Conclusion: 10 principles for digital transformation 199

ABOUT THE AUTHOR

Antonio Weiss, based in London, is a senior partner at The PSC, an award-winning public service consultancy specializing in user-centred design, digital, strategy and delivery. He has advised the Office for Artificial Intelligence, the UK Space Agency and NHSx as well as numerous other pioneering digital organizations, and he frequently trains leaders to become digital transformation experts. He is also an affiliated researcher at the University of Cambridge's Digital State programme and the co-founder of Thomas Clipper, an e-commerce lifestyle brand for men featured in *GQ*, the *Guardian* and the *Telegraph*.

ACKNOWLEDGEMENTS

This book is largely informed by my professional experiences over the past 15 years. I owe huge gratitude to the many wonderful clients I've worked with and also to my colleagues at The PSC, with whom I've shared so many good years. I'll spare the embarrassment of naming all, but would just like to particularly thank Phil Buckley and Katie Burns, who have been a source of inspiration and pleasure as we've worked together on many digital challenges over the years. My time as an affiliated researcher at Cambridge University's Bennett Institute Digital State programme helped broaden my international perspective and inform a number of the issues raised in this book.

Many friends from the world of digital transformation have helpfully reviewed and improved the book; particular thanks to Ben Crittenden for reading an early draft and offering invaluable comments on the sections on data science. Any errors, of course, are my own.

Kogan Page have been a delight to work with. I'm grateful to Amy and Chris for bringing me into the KP writing family and to Adam for his always speedy and attentive editing skills.

On a personal level, my wife, Carol has – as always – been hugely supportive of yet another writing project of mine. She and our boy, Frank, are a constant source of joy.

This book is dedicated to the memory of my wonderful friend Tom. We never got the chance to work together on the issues covered in these pages. But I know we'd have had a blast, even on the boring bits. Love you, buddy.

Introduction

Why you need this book

For anyone tasked with the job of 'digital transformation', we live in tricky times. On the one hand, there is a superabundance of books, blogs, podcasts and more covering new digital trends and fads which all promise to revolutionize the working world. On the other hand, particularly due to the huge changes wrought by Covid-19 and subsequent moves to significant remote working, everyone thinks they are a digital 'guru' now. Alas, one well-managed Zoom meeting does not make an expert. The reality is that the digital landscape is complex, messy, full of assertions and often bewildering. This book aims to help you cut through the noise to focus on what matters. In short: this book will help you know what to do to practically make digital transformation happen in your organization.

Before we get ahead of ourselves, let's start with some basics. What on earth do the words 'digital transformation' mean? You'll find endless, subtly different takes on this throughout the business literature, but for the purposes of this book you're holding, we are saying:

> Digital transformation means using the power of technology, data and digital services to change an organization or system for the better; to be more user-centred, more secure, and with a greater focus on delivering value to users, shareholders and wider society than ever before.

It's important to note that here we are using 'digital' as shorthand for digital services, data and technology. This is because since 'digital' has emerged from the shadows of 'information technology' or 'ICT' from the 2000s onwards, it has risked becoming confined to transactional services (think: 'accessing your bank details online') and the 'front-end' experience for customers. This is dangerous, because a great digital service needs to be truly integrated with the technology that runs the back end of the service and the data that underpins it. And so, throughout this book, we'll be considering all of these elements, as well as innovation, data science and analysis, and user-centred design.

Let's pause to consider what we mean by 'transformation' too. You can buy or build all the new fancy digital products and services in the world, but if no one in your organization uses them, and working processes don't change to benefit from the investments, then nothing will improve. Thus 'transformation' is a critical consideration throughout these chapters: how can you inspire, motivate and help your organization make the changes it needs to? While this book isn't focused on transformation *per se*, it unavoidably relates closely to it and you'll see references and advice on how to deliver change throughout.

Lastly, look at the outcomes in the second half of the 'digital transformation' description. Technology isn't inherently good. It's how we *apply* technology that can make our lives and the lives of others better. And so, we need to consciously consider this throughout. Technology needs to be focused on serving the needs of our users or customers, not ourselves; it needs to deliver real, tangible business benefits; and it needs to also be cognizant of the wider world. Digital can carry some unexpected nasty side effects. Biases demonstrated in machine learning algorithms which may result in prejudiced recommendations against black and ethnic minority groups is but one well-documented example. This book will help you navigate all of these issues.

What you'll know by the end

By the end of *The Practical Guide to Digital Transformation* you should be armed with:

- an understanding of the key concepts of digital transformation, how they can improve your business operations, and how to implement them successfully;
- a practical, proven methodology which leading digital organizations use;
- an assessment of the nature of your organization, and how to successfully transform it into one which makes best use of digital technologies to meet its goals;

- a clear appreciation of 'common pitfalls' to avoid when undertaking digital transformation;
- knowledge of who or where to turn to if you want to find out more about key topics.

How to read the book

This book is intended as a practical guide. While it's hopefully an enjoyable read, more than anything this book aims to be a primer to help you get your hands dirty and deliver actual, lasting digital transformation. As such, you can read it in one of two ways. First, as an end-to-end guide to accompany your digital transformation journey. It's structured to sequentially take you through the key stages of such a digital voyage. In Part 1, we focus on defining your digital strategy, choosing the vehicle for delivering the strategy, and then articulating the roadmap. In Part 2, we address the cultural aspects of great digital delivery. We'll work out how to fund your digital work, how to get your organization to buy in to the changes, and how to embrace agile ways of working. In Part 3, we cover the core fundamentals of great digital transformation: from adopting user-centred design to building or buying new services to adopting platform approaches and more. This is where we get into approaches that will help change your organization for the better. And in Part 4, we look to the future and consider how you can plan for future horizons, be an ethical organization and ensure you have the talent in-house to sustain your transformation. At the end, we'll summarize the learning with some key principles and a framework for analysis and considering digital technologies. The second way you can read this book is to dip in and out of the most relevant sections as and when you face these issues in your work. If you want to take this latter approach, you may wish to start with the Conclusion to give you a sense of the overarching principles of good digital transformation. The Appendix should also help to orientate you with some of the key terms from the digital world.

PART ONE

Getting the strategy and roadmap right

By failing to prepare, you are preparing to fail.

BENJAMIN FRANKLIN

Maybe it was a tap on the shoulder from the CEO. Or perhaps an unexpected email. Or maybe this was your dream job all along. Whichever way, someone, somehow has entrusted you to help the organization 'become digital'. Good luck.

You may not have a particularly strong digital or technology background, but you likely have a keen interest in the subject. It's likely that much of what you do know will be self-taught. That's great. This book isn't going to teach you how to code (arguably no book can – you just need to try it). But it should give you a clear sense of the fundamentals of digital transformation and how to put them into practice.

Whether you're inheriting a spaghetti of software systems and obsolete hardware or asked to create a technology blueprint from scratch, you will need to start with the basics. You need to get the digital strategy in place. Chapter 1 covers the first-order issues. What are you trying to achieve? How does it fit with the wider corporate strategy? Whose neck is on the line if this goes wrong? And why are you even doing this? You may think you already know all of this, but it's worth pausing and checking you do really have all the answers before steaming ahead. Get the strategy wrong and you're on the wrong track from the offset.

Chapter 2 addresses an underappreciated reality of transformation. All options are *not* open to you. A venture capital-backed Silicon Valley start-up founded by Stanford University data scientists will most likely have different means of delivering its digital strategy than a self-financed regional accountancy firm. Neither way is necessarily better. But it pays to be realistic. In this chapter you'll be given the tools to self-assess your organization and pick a winning strategic delivery vehicle accordingly.

In Chapter 3 we start getting into specifics. Working back from your strategic vision and with consideration of the vehicle at your disposal to get there, we break down the steps to form your digital roadmap. What do you do, and when? What is independent and what is interdependent? What will help you build momentum and what is hard but essential to do? The roadmap charts a path to achieve your vision. It won't be set in stone, but it will at least begin to point you in the right direction towards success.

01

What is a digital strategy?

Sure, everyone wants to 'do digital'. But why? What are you trying to achieve here? And how will you know if you're succeeding?

The principle in a nutshell

A digital strategy sets out the vision for an organization. It defines a small number of strategic options for how to deliver the vision and recommends a preferred option. The strategy must link directly to the organization's overall transformation objectives. Importantly, it must encompass all facets of 'digital': user needs, technology architecture, digital services and underpinning data flows.

A great strategy ties together the current state of an organization's digital maturity with its future ambition. It defines a clear and realistic timeframe for achieving the future ambition: essentially, how to get from A to B. There will always be different routes that organizations can take for realizing their ambitions: being an early adopter or fast follower, investing lots or investing the minimum, taking risks or being cautious. The digital strategy must consider such issues, evaluate them and propose a recommended way forward.

A digital strategy should be high-level. The detail comes once a preferred approach is agreed. The strategy should be easy to read for a non-technical audience. It should also be exciting and motivating. In an increasingly digital world, there are huge possibilities available to leverage technology to better meet the needs of citizens and customers in ways that were unimaginable until only recently.

What's the problem being addressed?

An effective digital strategy should help to address various common challenges organizations face:

- *Creating a seamless connection between corporate objectives and digital objectives:* a golden thread must run from an organization's overall objectives straight through the digital strategy. If it's not clear how an element of the digital strategy helps meet the overall goals of the organization, it probably shouldn't be part of the strategy.

- *Understanding why we need to change:* transformation is hard and if people reading the digital strategy don't understand why change is needed, it's unlikely they will embrace the new ways of working required. The strategy should set out – in stark terms, if required – why failing to change is not an option.

- *Reducing organizational silos:* a digital strategy *must* span across all parts of the organization. Digital cannot be boxed into a single unit or team – it affects everyone.

- *Prioritizing effort and resources:* the art of strategy involves realizing a future ambition with finite resources. A digital strategy should set out what gets delivered, and when. And importantly, what gets deprioritized.

- *Knowing if it's working:* teams and organizations need to know if delivery is on track. Setting measurable, realistic and demonstrable targets is vital.

- *Getting the right people involved:* studies into failed digital transformation invariably cite a 'lack of leadership' as a critical missing factor.[1] However, organizations need to ensure that digital strategies not only are well articulated and led, but also that they are sufficiently resourced to succeed.

Putting the principle into action

So where do you start? In the first instance, it's worth checking why you're even asking about a digital strategy. Whose job is it to create the digital strategy? What is your role in the organization? An effective digital strategy needs to be set by the senior leadership – we're talking board level – but implemented by all. If you're a chief digital/transformation/technology officer, you probably still need a mandate from your CEO and board colleagues to embark on devising a new digital strategy. If you're a head of/ senior manager and you know change is needed but the leadership in the organization is failing to act, you'll most likely need to influence and manage upwards – convincing the upper echelons why the organization needs to act.

There's no perfect time to develop a digital strategy, but there are often external or internal factors that make one highly advisable. These might include:

- change in senior leadership and vision;
- organization-wide transformation programmes being launched;
- expiring technology contracts;
- competitor organizations launching digital initiatives;
- customer expectations that far outstrip the reality of the service you currently give.

Launching a digital strategy because of one of these factors may seem a little reactive, but it's not necessarily a bad thing – there is already an in-built case for change. Proactively starting a new strategy in the absence of such factors may give you the luxury of time to think, but means you probably need to work harder to explain to colleagues why change is needed.

The value in setting out your thoughts in a simple and easy-to-follow manner should never be overestimated. Figure 1.1 sets out a 'strategic vision on a page' approach that you can use to guide your thinking.

Let's see how we can address each of these in turn. The *vision* for your digital strategy can be quite high-level, but let's aim to make it meaningful.

FIGURE 1.1 Strategic vision on a page

Vision *What are you aiming to achieve? In what timescale? How will it differentiate you from competitors?*	Leadership and resourcing *Who is ultimately accountable for the success or failure of this work? Who is leading the work on a day-to-day basis? Who is part of the team?*
Objectives *How will you measure success? Are your measurements tangible, timely and realistic?*	User needs *Who are your users? Are there internal and external users? What are their core needs from your organization?*
Case for change *Why are you doing this? And why are you doing this now?*	Risks and dependencies *What are the risks of doing this work? How does work relate to other things going on in your organization?*

There is a strong tendency for organizations to make such statements bland and uncontroversial, such as:

> We will leverage the power of digital, data and new technologies to improve our service to our customers.

Excited? Hardly. While the ambition is hard to argue with, it struggles to motivate or articulate what's special and unique about the organization's relationship to digital. Now let's imagine we're talking about a real estate agency looking to pivot from being a bricks and mortar high street company to one which serves customers digitally *and* through physical offices. How about the following vision?

> We will use the power of technology to provide an industry-leading digital experience for our customers, which blends seamlessly with their non-digital interactions with us.

Things are getting a bit more specific. *Industry-leading* provides a tangible level of ambition that we can measure and monitor. *Digital experience* demonstrates that we're aiming to go beyond transactional into a more two-way relationship with our customers. And *blends seamlessly* points to the need to integrate existing legacy operations with new digital operations. This vision is now both ambitious and meaningful. This can be used at a board level to quickly articulate what the digital strategy is aiming to achieve. And it expresses the vision in terms that are relevant to customers, demonstrating how the organization is seeking to make things better for them.

Setting *objectives* in the world of digital transformation is no different from good practice objective-setting elsewhere: we should aim to be specific, measurable, actionable, realistic and time-bound. This may need to be iterated as the organization decides on a specific strategic approach (of which more on this in Chapter 2), but putting down early thoughts is never a bad thing. Try to confine objectives to a small and manageable number. Continuing with our estate agency example, we might suggest:

- being ranked as one of the top three 'digital estate agents' nationally within five years;
- reducing overall operating costs by 20 per cent compared with current baseline in three years;
- implement a technology architecture that allows us to build and expand our service offering within two years.

The objectives here must – of course – tie in with overall corporate objectives. If there is already a cost-cutting ambition, this would be a good hook to link to. If there are national or industry rankings that are known and trusted, using these helps to avoid reinventing surveys. The final objective in this example is one that is extremely contingent on corporate objectives. If the organization is looking to expand its service offering (for example, by offering financial products to customers looking to move house or rent), ensuring technology can help to achieve this will be important. If the organization is looking to consolidate services instead, this would be irrelevant.

On the whole, most individuals in an organization will be resistant to change. Unless they are completely new in post, change will mean at best new behaviours and at worst may threaten their own employment prospects. As such, any successful strategy needs to be anchored in a clear response to the question, 'why do we need to change?' This is your *case for change*. This has to be pithy – you won't have long to convince sceptics. And you may need multiple ways of telling the story: personal anecdotes, hard facts and figures, and even graphics or memes can be powerful. Ultimately, most examples of a strong case for change boil down to a small number of variants:

- If we stay the same, costs will go up and our profitability will go down.
- Our competitors are racing ahead of us and our customers will leave us for them.
- Trends are emerging in our field that we need to adopt to survive.
- Regulations mean we have to change.
- Our workforce will leave if we don't address these issues.

Reflect on which one of these – or maybe more than one – is most relevant to your organization and tailor it, test how it works with friendly colleagues, and importantly, use specific evidence to your organization to bring it to life. It's important for all board members and senior leaders to speak as one on the case for change. Once you've refined it into something people are largely happy with, cascade the messages throughout the organization as you embark on the digital transformation journey (in Chapter 5 we learn more about how to get buy-in from the organization).

There tend to be two dreaded questions associated with transformation: who is on the hook for this, and who's delivering it? Tempting though it may be to fudge the issue of *leadership and resourcing*, you will quickly come to regret this. A digital transformation project with no leader and no team won't get very far.

In terms of leadership, you need to reflect on two issues. First, who is ultimately *accountable* for delivering the transformation? This should really be as senior as possible, ideally the chief executive, and certainly another C-level position. If the worst happens and the transformation fails, this is often the individual who carries the blame. Second, and arguably more importantly: who is *responsible* for the transformation? This is the person who is dedicated, on a day-to-day basis, to making the change a reality. Sometimes this is the same person, often not. Usual titles might be director of transformation, director of digital, etc. You might be this person.

And of course, you need *resourcing* to make this all a reality – change does not happen by magic. Depending on the strategic approach you take (see Chapter 2), you may be reliant on external suppliers or internal change teams or a mix. And the nature of the transformation will necessitate different levels of resourcing over differing timeframes. Your digital roadmap (covered in Chapter 3) will help in defining these needs, but it's critical these needs are articulated and met.

Since the early 2000s, one of the biggest changes in the world of information technology has been the focus on user-centred design (of which more in Chapter 7). Put simply, this means truly getting to know the people who your company serves, works with and relies on. By understanding *user needs*, organizations can avoid one of the most common technology pitfalls, which is to spend an eye-watering amount of money on software and hardware that nobody wanted or needed. Examples are plentiful, but consider the simple case of the BlackBerry smartphone. Lots of issues caused its demise, but one was the company's insistence on continuing to create devices with in-built keyboards. Competitors – notably Apple's early iPhones – demonstrated the fallacy that people 'needed' a keyboard, rather than a built-in touchscreen. Use a similar mindset to set out who the users of your organization are, and what they are truly aiming to achieve. We'll cover this in more detail later in the book, but it's good to start with an early view of this in your 'strategic vision on a page'. And remember – users are not just end-users such as your customers; they are also your internal staff, your suppliers and sometimes even your regulators.

And finally, make sure to be sighted on any glaring *risks and dependencies*. In the world of digital, there are often many. This is largely because digital is something that cuts across the operations of an organization. For instance, many organizations have or are looking to implement enterprise-wide customer relationship management platforms – essentially, software

TABLE 1.1 Digital risks and dependencies framework

	Risks	Dependencies
Internal	Organization capacity – do we have the time and headspace to do this? Resourcing and financing – do we have the money to do this? Capabilities – do we have the skills required?	What other changes are going on in the organization? When are they due? Who is involved in them? How will it affect the proposed changes in the digital strategy?
External	Are there any regulatory changes that may affect us? What are our competitors doing?	What changes in our industry may impact on our proposed changes?

that is used by the whole organization for a variety of purposes, from task identification and completion to customer contact or managing customer engagements. Such platforms affect everything from Finance to HR to front-line operations. Consequently, when you consider risks and dependencies for your digital strategy, think broadly. You may wish to reflect on the issues set out in Table 1.1, although there are many more candidates for things to consider.

Where next?

Your 'strategic vision on a page' should help to give you clarity on your thinking, but you may not have all the answers yet. That's to be expected. Depending on your role in the organization, you may wish to test the plans with colleagues in working groups or at a board session. Once you've got a board-level *accountable* individual on board and willing to sign off on the vision, your next step is to work out the strategic options available (Chapter 2) before moving onto the digital roadmap (Chapter 3).

BRINGING THE PRINCIPLE TO LIFE
A case study from the automotive world

In 2014, Mark Field, CEO of the American giant car manufacturer Ford, announced that the historic company would be moving into the markets of autonomous cars and electric vehicles. A new 'Ford Smart Mobility' Division was created to deliver on these plans, situated some thousands of miles from the company headquarters.

Ford's analysis of the case for change was compelling. Competitors such as Alphabet Inc. and Uber were investing heavily in driverless vehicle technology. And new trends such as car-sharing and green technologies were threatening Ford's operating model. However, by 2017 Field had been replaced by Jim Hackett and Ford's share price had declined by an arresting 40 per cent compared with three years previously. The Smart Mobility project was viewed as a failure – an attempt to undertake digital transformation entirely siloed from the rest of the core business of Ford. Employees were perceived to be unhappy at being separated from new initiatives (labelled as 'emerging' initiatives in the company), and the market and investors did not have confidence in Ford's ability to transform into a digital-first automotive company.[2]

As Bill Ford, the executive chairman of Ford, explained regarding the change of CEO to the media:

> You won't hear us talking [anymore], at least a lot, about emerging vs. core. This is one Ford Motor Co. We don't want one group to feel like they're the cool group and the other group is the left-out group. I think it's really important that we're seen by our employees and the public as 'This is the Blue Oval, this is how we're moving forward as a company,' and not as several companies.[3]

While the tale of the Smart Mobility Division at Ford may seem a simple, salutary warning against digital transformation being a siloed endeavour, the reality is more complex. As the late management strategist Clayton Christensen demonstrated, it's incredibly hard for established businesses to 'disrupt themselves' – or put another way, to transform how they work.[4] The operating models of established business are often hostile environments for new ways of working; overheads, estates and team structures may jar with proposed changes. There are really only two ways to address this that Ford could have taken. One way would have been to make the Smart Mobility Division an initially small innovation attempt, largely hidden from public gaze and with low expectations (see more in Chapter 13 on how to do innovation well). The alternative would have been to make digital transformation integral to the change – with the Smart Mobility Division not a separate entity, but an integrated part of Ford's way of working.

Tips and tricks

- Start with your organizational objectives. Think how digital technologies can help you meet these objectives, rather than the other way around.
- Work out who is ultimately on the hook for delivery of the digital transformation. If it's you, make sure you have board support and sign-off.

- Make sure there is a clear case for change. If there isn't, you'll struggle to engage people.

- Get your thoughts down early. Use the 'strategic vision on a page' to address the critical issues and test, refine and iterate until you're happy.

- Don't accept 'we can't afford to resource this' as an answer – change doesn't come for free.

What you might say in your next meeting

No change is not an option. Do we want to be known as the organization that 'bet against' digital?

We're not talking about an 'IT strategy' or 'technology roadmap'. Digital is all-encompassing and affects how each of us works.

We can't do this in silos. We need to work together, otherwise the digital transformation is guaranteed to fail.

If we don't resource this properly, it just won't happen. And we will all suffer as a result.

Our customers have the highest digital expectations now. If we fail to meet those, they'll go elsewhere.

Where you can find out more

For a masterful overview of what strategy is and where it comes from, try Lawrence Freedman's *Strategy: A History* (Oxford University Press, 2013). Helpful tools and frameworks abound in Max McKeown's *The Strategy Book* (Pearson, 2011). And an excellent example of a corporate digital strategy can be found in the Royal London Borough of Greenwich's 2020–2024 digital strategy.[5]

Notes

1 Anand, N and Barsoux, J-L (2017) What everyone gets wrong about change management. *Harvard Business Review*, Nov–Dec, hbr.org/2017/11/what-everyone-gets-wrong-about-change-management (archived at https://perma.cc/8APS-96LE)

2 Vlasic, B (2017) As Ford takes investor meeting online, brickbats still sting, *New York Times*, 1 May, www.nytimes.com/2017/05/11/business/ford-motor-shareholder-meeting.html (archived at https://perma.cc/4KL7-WSG7)

3 Martinez, M (2017) Where Mark Fields fell short, *Automotive News*, 22 May, www.autonews.com/article/20170522/OEM02/170529976/where-mark-fields-fell-short (archived at https://perma.cc/962C-PN4Q)

4 Christensen, C (1997) *The Innovator's Dilemma*, Harvard Business Review Press, Cambridge, MA

5 www.royalgreenwich.gov.uk/info/200222/policies_and_plans/2259/digital_strategy_2020_to_2024 (archived at https://perma.cc/GP6F-EGSL)

02

Choosing your strategic delivery vehicle

Vision and reality often create strategic tensions. Not every option is available to every organization. How can you be confident your strategy will suit your organization?

The principle in a nutshell

During the 2010s it became a commonplace in boardrooms across the working world to hear phrases such as 'how can we become the Netflix or Uber or Facebook of our sector?' While well intentioned and occasionally helpful, such conversations often overlooked the brutal reality that not all organizations are multi-billion-dollar valuation technology companies.

The success of a strategy will be contingent on many factors. The organization within which the strategy is enacted is of uppermost importance. When it comes to digital transformation, there are only a small number of viable ways that you can deliver a strategy that works: this is your 'strategic delivery vehicle'. It is the energy, the people, the money, the unit of change which will make your digital strategy a reality. But it needs to fit with the organization that it is trying to change. When assessing this 'strategic fit', be as objective as possible. By considering the real and emerging characteristics of the organization you work in, you can devise your strategy accordingly.

Consider this exercise as picking the 'vehicle' for your strategic journey. Whether you pick a scooter, a bicycle, an electric vehicle or a driverless train will depend on the scale of your resources, your appetite for risk and your time pressures. Once you know your chosen vehicle, you can then move on to planning the roadmap.

What's the problem being addressed?

Careful consideration of the alignment between your organizational type and the delivery vehicle for your strategy is an oft-forgotten but important part of successful digital transformation. By doing this, you are ensuring key ingredients are in place for success:

- *Avoiding culture clash:* a large transformation team, lavishly resourced with expensive consultants, is unlikely to sit well in an organization facing severe cost reduction pressures. Similarly, a bottom–up, decentralized approach may jar with a deeply hierarchical organization.

- *Being pragmatic about costs and resources:* change isn't free. Few organizations have a bottomless pit of financial reserves upon which they can infinitely call upon to support change efforts. Recognize the financial conditions you are working with, and plan accordingly.

- *Realism about your talent pool:* many organizations harbour a desire to create their own, bespoke and built in-house digital solutions. But, in an age of limited supply and high demand for digital skills, it may not be realistic to assume that your organization will be able to attract and retain the necessary talent to deliver in-house strategies.

- *Managing expectations:* one of the main reasons transformation efforts are cited to fail is because they fail to meet expectations. Of course, there are two sides to this, and you should address both: manage expectations about your strategy pragmatically so that you don't set off with too great presumptions that can burden your efforts before they've even started. And of course, make sure you deliver on these.

Putting the principle into action

Assessing your organizational archetypes

A *self-assessment* of your organization can help you to understand the critical factors that guide the choice of your strategic delivery vehicle. Table 2.1 can help you understand your organizational archetype.

First, consider the *centrality of technology to the value proposition of the organization.* For instance, while a chain of barbershops may use technology for important parts of its operations – social media for customer outreach, rotas for staffing, customer bookings and so forth – the main

TABLE 2.1 Organizational self-assessment

Self-assessment criteria	Questions to ask	Archetypes
Centrality of technology to the value proposition	• Is the main way your customers engage with your services through technology? • Do you call yourselves a technology company?	Tech-first vs Tech-enabled
Leadership	• Is there a chief technology or chief digital officer on the board? • Have they led successful digital transformation programmes before?	Digitally mature vs Digitally nascent
Organizational capabilities	• What was the last successful technology change that your organization undertook? • Does your organization have in-house digital capabilities?	In-house vs Externally reliant vs Mixed economy
Silos	• Is there regular collaboration across business units? • Are there frictions between senior leaders in the organization?	Siloed vs Multidisciplinary
Attitudes to failure	• What was the last change effort that failed? • How is the effort now viewed? Positively, because lessons were learned, or negatively, because it cost time and money?	Fail fast vs Just don't fail
Financial appetite	• What's the budget for the change effort? • How will the money be released?	Side of desk vs Pilot-first vs Bottomless pit
Technology legacy	• Do you have lots of existing software systems? • How easily does data flow between systems?	Brownfield vs Greenfield

value proposition of the barbershop is probably some combination of the quality of its barbers, the cost to clients, and its location and convenience. Technology is not really central to what it is or what it does. By contrast, for the online booking platform that the barbershops use, technology is at the core of the value proposition. This is significant because when choosing the delivery vehicle for those organizations for whom technology is central, these organizations should be careful in avoiding choosing a digital transformation vehicle that is entirely reliant on external suppliers. If you outsource your value proposition, you no longer have a value proposition.

The *leadership* of your organization matters to the delivery vehicle option. An organization with limited digital expertise at the top will need to entrust board-level responsibility for the transformation carefully. A deputy may be required to support the individual(s) chosen, to provide them with expertise that they lack. Relatedly, if internally *organizational capabilities* are demonstrably lacking and insufficient to deliver the strategic aims, they will need to be sourced either from new hires, agencies, consultancies or contractors.

The extent to which there are organizational *silos* also guides the shape of the transformation effort. A heavily siloed environment – one where business units and support functions seldom talk to each other, except when something goes wrong (and then it's probably too late to do something about it anyway) – may need something that helps to bridge the divides, rather than exacerbate them.

The business's *attitude to failure* is also instructive. Here, there may sometimes be a disconnect between reality and rhetoric. Since the 2000s and the rise of Facebook in particular, many leaders like to claim they embrace a 'fail fast' culture – one where experimentation is encouraged, and failure accepted as essential to eventually discovering success. But often the reality is divorced from this. Try and separate out the evidence as to whether your organization really tolerates and encourages iteration and trying things out. If it doesn't, you probably will need to be particularly cautious in your transformation efforts.

Financial appetite for change is critical. There are usually three types of finance director views on this subject: 'can't you do this side of desk?'; 'we'll pay for a pilot but then write me a business case'; and 'we'll pay whatever it takes'. None is perfect. The first is impractical, the last is implausible and the middle one can be bureaucratic. But you will most likely work in one of these environments and need to adjust as necessary.

And finally, the *technology legacy* that you are bequeathed will determine whether you are a 'brownfield' (lots of old systems and technology) or 'greenfield' (a clean slate) site. Most organizations, bar start-ups, are brownfield and one of the main reasons why all the Silicon Valley analogies ('we can be the Spotify of construction') don't work.

To complete the self-assessment, *use* a number of different approaches. The questions to ask in Table 2.1 are by no means comprehensive, but merely a guide. You'll find answers in interviews with colleagues, reading through your company's strategy or annual reports, reflecting on your own day-to-day working practices, and talking to friends working for other employers. Sometimes comparing your own experiences with someone else's can shed new light on your understanding. As you complete the questions, you should be able to select the different *archetypes* that represent your organization.

Let's take an example. There is an independent sector chain of care homes that has been running for 80 years. It has a small executive team, led by a chief executive, finance director and chief operating officer. None of them have a strong technology background. The company's operations are primarily physical – caring for residents – and while technology helps in staff rostering, HR appraisals and finance, beyond a website, most customers don't have a particularly strong digital experience with the care home. That said, there's certainly scope for some innovation – video calls with residents, resident-tracking and so forth. The care home has grown from several mergers over the years, and so various software and hardware have been stitched together over time. There was a large transformation programme a few years ago to create a 'One Caring' culture and generate efficiencies – this was led by a big consultancy firm. The programme is believed to have been a failure by the senior leadership, and the individual who led the transformation is no longer employed by the care group.

How would you assess a business like this? From what we know – and you would wish to do more investigating to be certain – it sounds like the care home chain has the archetypes of: tech-enabled (because technology supports caring for residents, but caring isn't delivered by technology); digitally nascent (due to the lack of senior digital leadership); probably externally reliant on technology suppliers (if the transformation programme is anything to go by); probably siloed (because the 'One Caring' culture programme failed and there have been lots of mergers); home to a 'just don't fail attitude' (given that the transformation lead seems to have been ushered out after the programme); financial appetite is unclear, but probably 'side of desk' or 'pilot first' (if the finance director is so central to the leadership and the transformation programme was focused on efficiencies); and the technology landscape sounds pretty 'brownfield' (given the stitching together of IT systems). This is just a rapid assessment, but this can give a great start when we consider: what strategic delivery vehicle should the care group choose?

Choosing the strategic delivery vehicle

How to deliver great transformation and change programmes has been written about extensively elsewhere. At the end of this chapter, you'll find some references to some good resources. Instead, here we will focus less on transformation in general and more on the specifics of how to do digital transformation. Notwithstanding, a few key principles are always worth reiterating:

- Transformation needs to be led from the top of the organization, but supported and understood by everyone in the organization.
- Transformation needs to be properly funded and resourced, with dedicated time and effort outside of 'business as usual'.
- Transformation requires skills and capabilities that may need to be brought into the organization.

While these principles need to be adhered to, when it comes to digital transformation, there are a number of different angles one can take when developing the vehicle to deliver the strategy. Six considerations can help guide us.

LEAD INNOVATOR VERSUS FAST FOLLOWER

Organizations which are 'lead innovators' take risks, aim to go to market first with new products and services, and typically spend a good amount of corporate time on outward-facing communications explaining to others how brilliant they are. They often win prizes and their leaders gain great reputations. But lead innovators also fail frequently. They often spend money inefficiently as they churn through ideas that don't survive. And for every industry-leading organization, there are scores more that tried to be lead innovators but failed. Organizations with a strong *fail-fast* mentality, who have a *bottomless financial pit* to support change and are *digitally mature* with strong *in-house* digital capabilities are those most likely to succeed. But be warned. Even with these in place, they may not.

'Fast followers' are by turn more cautious. They wait to see what works and then look to copy it. On the well-known 'innovation lifecycle' you might consider them anywhere between 'early adopters' and 'late majority' (perhaps even an element of 'laggard'.) This is a recommended position for organizations that are *digitally nascent*, where finances are more *business case*-constrained and there is a fear of failure and risk-taking.

Organizations which are *brownfield* sites will struggle to become lead innovators. It is not impossible, but the sheer bulk of legacy technology that will have to be updated, upgraded or amended in order to let innovation thrive will provide a significant overhead. *Greenfield* sites, unencumbered by historic technology decisions, may thrive more as innovators.

CENTRALIZED VERSUS DECENTRALIZED

If we think of transformation as a unit of energy, the consideration here is where in the organization does this energy best lie? Is it in a central team, closely guarded by executives, or is it dispersed throughout the organization? **Digitally mature organizations** with **in-house** digital capabilities spread throughout the organization and a positive *fail-fast* attitude are more likely to succeed with a 'decentralized' model. However, organizations which don't possess these characteristics, and particularly those which are badly *siloed* invariably benefit from a 'centralized' model. With centralized models, the aspiration should be to push responsibility for transformation delivery throughout the whole organization, but the bulk of energy should sit centrally. A good example of this would be a digital transformation team that reports directly to the chief executive but deploys teams across different units in an organization.

FUNDING POT VERSUS BUSINESS CASES

Paying for digital transformation can take two archetypes: establishing a transformation 'funding pot' where money is committed and protected for a finite period of time; or creating a stage-gate 'business case' approach, where money is released contingent on business cases being written and approved at set intervals. Organizations with a *bottomless pit* financial mentality and a *fail-fast* attitude may well benefit from the 'funding pot' approach. For all others, at least putting in place some rigour of stage-gates is recommended. However, be careful with the balance here; you don't want expensive or in-demand digital resources spending all their time writing business cases. We cover more about approaches to funding digital effectively in Chapter 6.

AGILE VERSUS WATERFALL

We'll talk more about this throughout this book, but in short, while *digitally nascent* organizations probably prefer a waterfall approach – think Gantt charts, project plans and sequential delivery planning – almost no digital projects are recommended to be delivered this way. This is because digital projects almost always involve a degree of innovation, uncertainty and complexity, which means guaranteeing deliverables by certain timelines is, at best, foolhardy. Adopting an agile approach to delivery (see Chapter 4) will help with managing budgets and expectations. That said, if your organization is *externally reliant* on technology skills, be careful to manage the suppliers closely; it's fine for them to deliver in an agile fashion, but they need to meet their contractual commitments to you, and so putting in place an element of waterfall 'stage-gates' would be recommended.

SINGLE SUPPLIER VERSUS MIXED ECONOMY

This trade-off is largely about the technical architecture of your organization. Organizations that choose to rely on a single enterprise platform, for instance, should really only be those that are *tech-enabled*; by committing to a single supplier, you are effectively putting all of your eggs in one basket. If your systems fail, your ability to fulfil your core value proposition goes with it. It is often also harder to tailor certain systems to meet end-user needs with a single supplier; expensive developer teams and resources are likely to be needed. A *mixed economy* that involves a number of suppliers and platforms may give you greater flexibility and autonomy if you are a *tech-first* organization.

IN-HOUSE VERSUS EXTERNAL CAPABILITIES

Once changes brought by the digital transformation become embedded in your organization, should you develop in-house digital expertise or rely on external support? Again, the extent to which you are a *tech-first* or *digitally mature* organization should guide you here: those organizations which are both *tech-first* and *digitally mature* should look to develop strong internal capabilities. Those which are not will probably struggle to recruit such skills, and as such are better to rely on them as and when they are needed.

Where next?

By completing the self-assessment and determining the strategic vehicle that will best suit your organization, you have decided the shape of your transformation approach. You have your vision and strategy and vehicle now agreed. But you don't have the details of exactly what you want to do, and by when. The next step is to break down your digital vision into discrete goals and develop a roadmap (Chapter 3). There is inevitably an element of iteration here. If your roadmap is hoping to lead you to a place where your organization shifts from being tech-enabled to tech-first, you may wish to revisit your considerations about your strategic delivery vehicle. These aren't rules set in stone and judgements should always apply. But they should guide you on the next phase of the journey.

BRINGING THE PRINCIPLE TO LIFE
Innovating government publishing and the UK Government Digital Service

At the start of the 2010s it was a commonly held view that British government did not do technology very well. Perceived disaster stories, such as the £12 billion NHS Connecting for Health programme, were frequently cited by politicians as examples of the state's inability to deliver digital transformation. With over 500 public sector bodies and over 20 central government departments, getting a grip on delivery was no easy task.[1]

In October 2010, Martha Lane-Fox, co-founder of the British internet travel site lastminute.com and UK Digital Champion, wrote a letter to the then Prime Minister David Cameron and Minister for the Cabinet Office Francis Maude calling for a 'revolution, not evolution' in how government approached digitization, specifically focusing on its approach to publishing information and providing services to citizens. Lane-Fox also noted how 'leadership on the digital communications and services agenda is too fragmented' and that a new CEO for Digital needed to have 'absolute authority over the user experience across all government online services', which totalled hundreds of websites. In short, Lane-Fox was describing an extremely *siloed* ecosystem, but one where transactional services – such as car tax, student loans, or job search – could make government services *tech-first* in terms of the centrality of technology to the user experience.[2]

With this in mind, Lane-Fox proposed a core central team, reporting directly to the Minister for the Cabinet Office, which was to become the UK Government Digital Service (GDS) in 2011. This model of strategic delivery vehicle was effectively a *lead innovator* unit, highly *centralized*, working in *agile* ways and with significant *in-house* capabilities. This model – now known as Digital Government Units – has been replicated worldwide, with similar units found in Canada, the US, Chile, Argentina and beyond. While the successes of GDS – particularly in the development of the single Gov.UK publishing platform, which replaced 2,000 government websites with just one user-friendly and accessible site – have been much lauded, the model is not without criticisms: that it alienates those individuals outside of the core team and that it is less effective in highly *brownfield* sites. However, it remains a prime example of a strategic delivery vehicle that diagnosed the current state and culture of the environment it was seeking to change and succeeded accordingly.[3]

Tips and tricks

- Use the self-assessment exercise to be dispassionate and objective about your organization; by recognizing your environment's traits and culture, you'll be in a better position to deliver your transformation aims.
- Test your assessment with trusted colleagues. If their views differ, discuss why and consider amending your conclusions.
- Remember to sense-check your preferred strategic delivery vehicle with your roadmap intentions. Once you know what you're planning on doing and when, does it change your thinking about the vehicle?
- There are no right or wrong delivery vehicles – just different choices to be made.
- Don't forget all the good principles of successful transformation – digital transformation is still transformation.

What you might say in your next meeting

Please don't ask 'how can we be like Facebook?' We're not Facebook.

We have our vision; now we need to work out how we're going to get there.

Transformation involves making hard decisions: we can't be all things to all people. We need to work with the grain of our existing culture.

How central is technology to our value proposition to customers? If it's key, we need to be much more in control of our technological destiny than we are currently.

This won't come cheap. So let's be realistic about what we can afford.

Where you can find out more

There is a large literature on change management and transformation which has helped inform the thinking in this chapter on delivery vehicles. John Kotter is rightly regarded as one of the leading – and most accessible – writers on the topic. His *Leading Change* (Harvard Business Press, 2013) and *Our Iceberg is Melting* (Macmillan, 2014) are excellent guides. Chip Heath's *Switch* (Random House, 2010) is particularly strong on some of the softer elements of change.

Notes

1   Weiss, A (2019) *The Rise and Fall of UK Digital Government: Learning from the past*, Cambridge University Bennett Institute for Public Policy, 9 October, www.bennettinstitute.cam.ac.uk/blog/rise-and-fall-uk-digital-government/ (archived at https://perma.cc/R3A2-C8RB)

2   *A GDS Story*, Government Digital Service, gds.blog.gov.uk/story/ (archived at https://perma.cc/H3XE-YUT9)

3   UK House of Commons: Science and Technology Committee (2019) *Digital Government*, 3 July, publications.parliament.uk/pa/cm201719/cmselect/cmsctech/1455/1455.pdf (archived at https://perma.cc/U5V6-GBCM)

03

How to do a digital roadmap

You've got your vision. You know how you hope to get there.
But what are the precise steps you need to take next?
Your digital roadmap will help answer this.

The principle in a nutshell

Becoming 'digital' doesn't happen by magic. To give yourself the best chance of success, you need a carefully considered, well-articulated plan for how you get from where you are now to where you want to be. This is your digital roadmap.

Somewhat paradoxically, while you need to aim to stick faithfully to your roadmap, you should also be very alive to the possibility that you may need to tweak it, amend it or rip it up and start again. This is at the heart of good agile working (see Chapter 4 for more). But it's also the essence of digitization. The changes you are planning may be so novel, or the technologies you are adopting so rapidly developing, that the future is bathed in uncertainty.

So develop your roadmap with thought and care. Treat it as the glue between your vision, your strategic delivery vehicle and your desired end goal. Use the roadmap – which is likely to take the form of a written and, ideally, visually compelling document – to communicate to your seniors, your stakeholders and your colleagues. Celebrate your progress as you go. But it's always OK to change if circumstances require it. Just make sure to develop a new roadmap when you do.

What's the problem being addressed?

A roadmap is a vital artefact for any digital transformation. It speaks to multiple audiences: senior stakeholders, team members and even customers. And it serves multiple important purposes:

- *Aligning your vision with your strategic delivery vehicle:* the roadmap helps make real the 'what' that you're aiming to achieve with the 'how' for which you're planning on doing it. It is your plan, and if the plan doesn't match the vision, it won't work.

- *Communicating what you're doing:* it is essential that you are transparent with the organization as to what the digital transformation entails. The roadmap should have multiple layers of detail, but at the highest level, it should be able to quickly inform a senior audience exactly what to expect, and by when.

- *Avoiding doing everything at once:* failure to prioritize will simply lead to failure. Roadmaps force you to set what you will do first and then the sequence of what comes next. A roadmap should also help you understand what could be dropped altogether. If a workstream or initiative doesn't clearly help you achieve your vision, don't do it.

- *Working out the interdependencies:* any change involves workstreams that are interdependent. And this is particularly true in the world of technology. You may be planning on implementing an analytics service – but does the analytics solution need to integrate with your main enterprise platform? It most probably does, and so you should put determining the platform first in your roadmap and only then deciding on the analytics solution. By understanding the interdependencies (and also what is therefore *independent* – not connected to other decisions), you'll be able to narrow down options and be clearer about the phasing of key decisions.

- *Setting checkpoints to track progress:* a good roadmap should set out outcomes and deliverables to be achieved within a given timeframe. As you progress through the lifespan of your roadmap, you can check in on progress.

- *Allowing opportunities to pivot:* and of course, if you are well off track from your plan, your roadmap should present opportunities where you can change course before it's too late.

Putting the principle into action

So this is when your digital strategy starts to become real. You will have already developed your strategic vision and have stated objectives. You should also have a strong sense of the strategic delivery vehicle you want to get you there. Now we want to outline the specific steps that will help to form the roadmap. By the end you should have a clear plan for a defined time period, with detail that describes the workstreams, objectives, outcomes and individuals delivering the roadmap components. The following steps will guide you.

1. Start with the strategic vision and timeframes

With guidance from Chapter 1, you should have detailed what you're trying to achieve, and very importantly, set yourself a timescale for achieving it. A roadmap should ideally be no more than five years, and usually a sub-three-year horizon is optimal. This reduces uncertainty and avoids creating too many 'potential' different paths to take. If your organizational strategy, as many organizations do, is looking at something more akin to a ten-year timeframe, consider dividing the time into 'horizons' of three-year chunks. This should stop you from making wild assumptions by presupposing that you can know the future.

Let's consider a worked example here. In early 2020 as a result of the Covid-19 pandemic, many restaurants had to rapidly pivot towards becoming digital restaurants – offering home deliveries, bookings, remote payments and more. In this scenario, a digital vision could have been something about 'enabling a first-class dining experience underpinned by digital technology from the comfort of our customer's home *or* our safe and Covid-secure restaurants, within three months'.

2. Establish the user needs

We will cover this in more detail in Chapter 7; however, the importance of using actual users – customers, staff, stakeholders, shareholders – to guide your strategy cannot be overstated. You should set out who your key users are, and then what the 'needs' – the things that they want to achieve or obtain through using your service – of these users are. This should be future-facing, so you may include 'needs' that are not currently served by your current state, but which you are aiming to achieve.

In our restaurant example you might have:

- As a *current customer*, I want to be able to order, pay for, track delivery of and give feedback on my food order, so that I can enjoy my order at home.
- As a *potential customer*, I need to know what the restaurant offers so that I can consider whether to place an order.
- As a *staff member*, I need to know what the orders are so that I can fulfil them.
- As a *restaurant administrator*, I need to know what was ordered, when, and that it was paid for, so that I can process accounts and payments.

There may be more needs – for instance, customers may wish to make a booking for the restaurant or administrators may wish to understand business performance through analytics – but these give an idea of some key user needs.

3. Develop the workstreams and cross-reference with the delivery vehicle

By understanding user needs you can begin to shape workstreams that meet these needs. In the above example, you may determine you have four broad workstreams:

- serving current customers;
- winning new customers;
- digitizing internal operations;
- reporting and analytics.

These should roughly match, respectively, the order of the user needs described above. While you should not be jumping to a solution yet – the following chapters will help you decide on the best solution – your strategic delivery vehicle will set parameters for you. For example, going back to our restaurant case study, let's assume that the restaurant has decided it is best to take a *fast follower*, *centralized*, *single supplier* and *external capabilities* reliant model, owing to the digital immaturity of the organization and the fact that technology is not one of its core competencies. This should help narrow the options available quite materially: with these organizational archetypes in mind, the restaurant would be wise to choose a single software platform to fulfil as many of its user needs as possible.

4. Cluster the interdependencies

In some instances, one technology choice will close down options for future choices. Shopify, one of the biggest ecommerce platforms, has a large range of API-enabled connections to a suite of applications for everything from mailing list management to analytics. But it doesn't cover everything. With this in mind, if you choose Shopify over another ecommerce platform such as Stripe, your options will be restricted by your original platform choice: these are *interdependencies*. In your roadmap, try and disentangle where you have interdependencies. Again, in our restaurant example, it's likely that the 'reporting and analytics' workstream will be dependent on the software decisions made for 'serving current customers'. Here it would consequently be important to make the decision for this latter workstream first.

5. Identify the fixed points

Are there any critical changes or issues in your timeframe that you need to factor into your plans? In Europe, changes to data security requirements such as the 2018 General Data Protection Regulation (GDPR) Act ensured all companies processing customer data had to factor in GDPR compliance into their roadmaps. Other common issues that create fixed points are cloud hosting decisions (see Chapter 11) or re-platforming. On the former, for example, certain hosting domains – of which Microsoft Azure or Amazon Web Services are the most common – may have an impact on your software choices. A number of analytics tools are better suited to one cloud environment than another, for instance. Consequently, if there are organizational plans to move to a given cloud hosting platform at a specific date, factor this into the roadmap – it may cause you to delay certain workstreams.

6. Cost up and prioritize

In Chapter 6 we go into some detail on the funding and financing of digital projects. However, even at this early stage, you should be looking to have a broad sense of how much certain workstreams will cost. Ascertaining costs should be guided by the decisions you've made regarding your strategic delivery vehicle. If you're going for a single supplier approach, some early pre-procurement conversations with potential suppliers, or speaking to similar organizations using the suppliers you're considering should give you an early idea of costs. If you're planning on developing your own digital services, you should have a broad sense of development costs and be able to factor in rough timings. Make sure to include any costs related to organizational changes (see Chapter 4 for more details).

Once you've set out the likely costs, you may need to prioritize workstreams or even hold some back. In our restaurant example, while you may strongly wish to onboard new potential customers with a social media drive, the costs of a large digital campaign may cause you to delay this until the most pressing changes are up and running.

7. Set out the roadmap and governance

Once you have your workstreams prioritized, you should be in a position to write out the roadmap and develop its phasing. For each step in the roadmap, consider:

- What are you trying to do? eg, develop a digital customer buying, tracking and feedback experience;
- When does it need to be done by? eg, end of quarter 1;
- Who is doing it? eg, digital innovation team, supported by seconded restaurant staff input;
- What are the key outcome measures? eg, 95 per cent+ client satisfaction in process.

You may consider that some parts of the roadmap should be piloted first. If so, make this clear, and then specify what are the success criteria for the pilot and what happens if it's successful or unsuccessful.

The roadmap will need supporting governance. Ultimate responsibility and accountability should have been addressed in Chapter 1, but you should also set out a steering group or project board to review progress and delivery against the roadmap, and ensure you have a feedback route up to senior stakeholders if challenges are encountered.

8. Communicate, communicate, communicate

And finally, do not hide the roadmap away. This should be a living, breathing and iterated document. It should become well known across your organization. Seek feedback on it early on. And then celebrate successes as you progress. This will help to build confidence in your ability to deliver and win trust through transparency and openness. The roadmap doesn't just

FIGURE 3.1 Example high-level roadmap

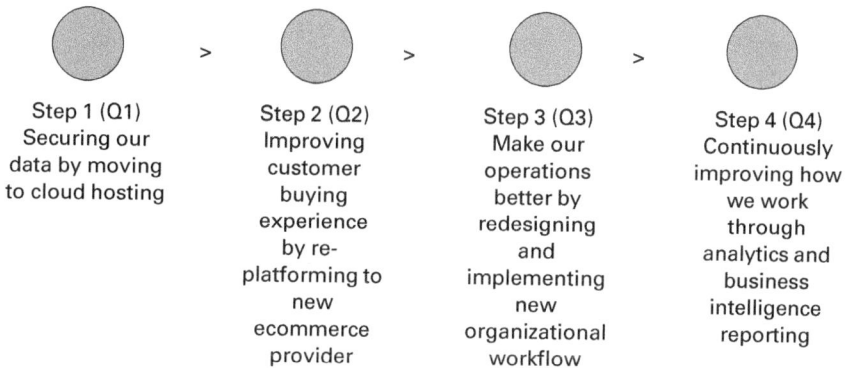

| Step 1 (Q1) Securing our data by moving to cloud hosting | > | Step 2 (Q2) Improving customer buying experience by re-platforming to new ecommerce provider | > | Step 3 (Q3) Make our operations better by redesigning and implementing new organizational workflow | > | Step 4 (Q4) Continuously improving how we work through analytics and business intelligence reporting |

need to be an internal document. Unless there are competitive reasons not to, think about sharing it publicly with customers – they may be keen and excited to know what future improvements they can expect from your organization.

By the end of these stages, you should be left with something that resembles Figure 3.1. More detail should sit underneath all of these steps, with this view designed for senior, time-poor, stakeholders in mind.

Where next?

The roadmap should leave you armed for success. However, we've covered a lot of ground and you may feel you don't have all the answers to the questions your roadmap asks just yet. Don't worry – this is to come in Parts 2 and 3 of the book, where we start to tackle the specifics. So, develop your roadmap, test it with your key stakeholders. Iterate where necessary, and prepare to get your hands dirty as we move into the delivery side of digital transformation.

BRINGING THE PRINCIPLE TO LIFE
A roadmap for moving from physical retail to digital ecommerce

Thomas Clipper is a British fragrance house, specializing in men's colognes. Founded in London in 2014, it initially targeted premium retailers as the main route for both selling to customers and for being discovered by new customers. The team had a clear roadmap to expand its physical retail presence, which it executed from 2014 to 2018, and built up an offering in over 50 retailers across a dozen countries.[1]

However, as the company sought to grow in scale and profitability, it made a strategic decision to move away from physical retail environments towards digital ecommerce. Reflecting on its internal archetypes, the Thomas Clipper founders decided that technology needed to be at the heart of the value proposition. As such, the team decided to go for a mixed-economy approach to digital development, run in an agile fashion and highly centralized.

When deciding on the roadmap, it was clear that the team was grappling with three core users: new and potential customers, who wanted a seamless end-to-end purchasing experience *and* to discover more about the products they owned; internal logistic operator users, who needed to know what to send and where; and senior management, who wanted to use data to monitor and continuously improve the operations of the business.

All three user needs and workstreams were heavily interdependent on the choice of ecommerce platform; both reporting analytics and warehouse integration choices were contingent on the initial platform choice. As such, the customer needs workstream was prioritized first, with internal and senior management needs subsequently run in parallel.

The digital transformation was successful. Within the first year of the roadmap being implemented, online sales increased by over 200 per cent and financial profitability by nearly the same amount, as fewer physical retailers meant the company kept the previous margin that physical retailers would take off sales. The company was featured as a leading fragrance house by British *GQ* magazine. However, Thomas Clipper also noted some changes to its operating model that were unanticipated at the start of the digital transformation. Distributing abroad had become harder – responsibility for direct to customer shipment now lay with the company, rather than with third parties, which added unexpected costs. And customer acquisition now sat firmly with the company – digital advertising costs needed to increase as fewer customers were seeing products in retail outlets, as the company stripped back its retail presence. These reflections allowed the company to generate the next phase of its roadmap after the first key steps were implemented: to focus on digital advertising and marketing, and improve digital operations for internal shipments and distribution.

This agile approach to roadmap development allowed Thomas Clipper to continuously innovate and stay abreast of changes in its business operations. As co-founder Matt Brown stated:

> Making the change to being a digital-first company made complete sense. We could be closer to our customers by removing intermediaries. We improved financial efficiency and were able to scale operations more easily. However, it

came with some unforeseen impacts, and we were careful to factor into our roadmap planning not looking too far ahead, as we knew that we'd need to adjust as we learned more about our new operating model.'[2]

Tips and tricks

- Start with the end goal in mind. Your roadmap is about bridging the gap between getting there and where you are now.
- The roadmap should be a pruning exercise. If everything you ever dreamt of doing is in it, ask yourself if you're trying to do too much.
- The world of technology is messy and interlinked. One software or hardware choice is likely to constrain or impact on others' choices. Try to have a clear sense of where the linkages are and pre-empt them in your roadmap planning.
- Don't be afraid to iterate your roadmap as you go. You will inevitably learn more than you knew at the start and should embrace this newly discovered knowledge.
- Make the roadmap intelligible to a lay person. This should be a key artefact to communicate to people what your digital transformation is all about.

What you might say in your next meeting

We have a vision. Now we need to set out how we're going to get there.

The roadmap needs to be coherent with our strategic delivery vehicle.

Let's not rush into snap decisions – a single bad choice here could minimize our options significantly further down the line.

Everything needs to start with what our users actually want: this will guide the roadmap.

Want to know what we're up to? Let me share our roadmap with you.

Where you can find out more

While the principles of good roadmaps should be pretty clear by now, there is actually surprisingly little in the way of literature that points to best-practice examples. The best suggestion is to be on the lookout for plans and roadmaps and see what resonates with you. Evaluate them for insightfulness, ease of interpretation and memorability. During 2021 many countries across the world adopted roadmaps to guide the public through the lifting of restrictions placed on society due to Covid-19. You may find it useful to go through some of these and see which you feel were most effective in terms of communications and, where appropriate, borrow some of their characteristics for your roadmap.

Notes

1 Coleman, A (2016) The luxury market is tricky to crack but the rewards can be great, *The Guardian*, 20 October, www.theguardian.com/small-business-network/2016/oct/20/luxury-market-entrepreneur-tricky-rewards (archived at https://perma.cc/EHX3-4UUZ)
2 Matt Brown expressed this statement in a call with the author on 10 March 2021.

PART TWO

Making change happen

Everyone has a plan until they get punched in the mouth.

MIKE TYSON

You've set your vision. You've got your roadmap. You've got a plan to deliver it. Plain sailing from now, right? Sadly, the real world has got a nasty surprise for your best-laid plans. Remember, digital transformation is fundamentally about *change*. And most people and most institutions struggle badly with change.

Three factors commonly come up when reasons for transformation failures are cited: inflexible working cultures; organizational hostility, especially from senior leaders; and a lack of funding and resourcing. In Part 2, we cover techniques for addressing each of these factors to give you the best chance of success in your digital transformation efforts.

In Chapter 4 we cover what agile – which has been so influential in software development and engineering since the 2000s – can teach us about successful transformation approaches. How can user-centred approaches make your organization more efficient? What does a great digital team look like? And how can you showcase your new ways of working to the wider organization? In this chapter, we'll also address some of the pitfalls you need to watch out for while becoming more agile.

You can have the most effective digital team and a great, dynamic and agile culture, but if the seniors and executives in your organization don't believe in the transformation, *it will fail*. What can you do to deal with this? In Chapter 5 we cover what approaches and techniques you can use to win over key stakeholders and manage – and hopefully change the minds of – the doubters who don't want to see you succeed.

And finally, digital doesn't come for free. Computing and processing power may be increasing exponentially, but it hasn't become exponentially cheaper. If you want to be a leading digital organization, you need to fund this accordingly. But finance colleagues – so often burned by failed change projects – will probably start from a point of profound scepticism. In Chapter 6, we cover how to address these concerns, and describe effective ways of funding digital.

04

Ways of working

Everyone says we need to be 'agile' in how we work. But what does this mean? And what are the risks arising from new ways of working that you need to manage?

The principle in a nutshell

While many of the principles that underpin 'agile' ways of working pre-date its publication, a 2001 book called the *Manifesto for Agile Software Development* marked the start of a rapid swell of interest in agile approaches.[1] The book, developed over a weekend skiing trip in the Wasatch Mountains of Utah by 17 software developers and engineers, sought to address the problems they viewed in traditional ways of working in business: rigid project management approaches, a lack of focus on the customer, and too much paperwork and bureaucracy.

Emphasizing flat hierarchies, iterative approaches and a focus on multi-disciplinary team profiles, agile has rapidly become the preferred way of working for almost all leading technology companies, and many other firms have also sought to adopt its approaches. Banking, retail, education, health-care – you'd be hard pressed to find an industry that has not adopted agile ways of working in some form or another. Even if your organization is not a technology company, there are huge benefits you can reap from becoming more agile. But beware, as you may well have experienced, since the 2000s a zealotry has developed around agile ways of working that itself can make firms inflexible and bureaucratic. To get the most from agile, consider the component parts that form an agile culture, and then carefully adopt – and if necessary, adapt – those parts to your own organization. Agile in general is great, but it's not for everyone, all the time.

What's the problem being addressed?

Agile is most commonly understood as operating in distinction from 'waterfall' project management disciplines and organizational cultures. Waterfall, somewhat crudely, is characterized by linear, sequential project management (think Gantt charts or Microsoft Project Plan) techniques which presuppose that the world is knowable, certain and plannable. While this may be true if you're building a bridge – although even then, supply chain issues or labour availability mean nothing is truly certain – the theory goes that this is far from true if you're building or implementing new digital services or technologies. The point is that they are new and therefore how your organization reacts to the new technologies or challenges in development and implementation are unknowable. Agile approaches are therefore particularly helpful in:

- *Managing risk and uncertainty:* agile involves setting an end goal and then establishing the 'known' elements you have at your disposal to get there; time, resources and cost. By doing so, you can be clearer about the process with stakeholders and set checkpoints along the way. Rather than commit to do everything by a certain date some way in the future, agile involves agreeing incremental steps and openly demonstrating progress against these, or highlighting challenges as they arise.

- *Bringing the best of the organization together:* great agile teams are multidisciplinary in nature. This is true in both a functional sense – a digital team should have more than just software developers; it needs user researchers and service designers, a product manager and more (see Chapter 16 for the skills needed) – it is also true in a sectoral or geographic sense. Agile team members should represent *all* relevant parts of the organization.

- *Working at pace:* agile working patterns are described as 'sprints'. This is no misnomer. A sprint is a short, snappy period of time – usually one or two weeks. It is full of daily and weekly rituals, as well as a full-on work schedule. Ideally, agile team members are fully committed and dedicated to the work.

Putting the principle into action

Don't worry too much about whether you are fully committing as an organization to 'agile' or 'waterfall' ways of working. This will just lead to heated debates, existential questions about 'corporate culture' and create unnecessary divides. Instead, as you set about delivering your *digital roadmap* (Chapter 3), make sure you embrace the following principles and ways of working.

Putting the user at the heart of how you work

Chapter 7 covers this in-depth, but in terms of importance, being 'user-centred' is by far the most important approach you can adopt in order to undertake digital transformation effectively. In short, user-centricity – also known as 'human-centred design' – is about understanding what different people want and need from the products and services your organization delivers. Most people think about users as being *external* to your organization – customers, suppliers, regulators, etc – but they are also *internal* too – staff members, managers, and so on.

Being user-centred involves going and speaking to these people, getting clear on how they actually experience your organization and using technology to either improve their experiences or make much better experiences. User-centricity should be considered as being in contrast to the phrase 'serving the beast'. For example, filling in duplicative forms 'because HR wants me to' is the opposite of user-centred; the forms serve the needs of the organization, not the user. User-centricity should mean that your users have as simple and seamless an experience as possible.

Iterating towards your end goals

Your roadmap will have broken down your end vision (Chapter 1) into more discrete goals that form the steps of your roadmap. Each step can be treated like its own workstream, with its own end goal. For example, if your roadmap has a specific workstream of 'roll out new enterprise resource planning (ERP) software across the organization', having the ERP in every business unit in the organization might be your end goal. Adopting an agile approach would mean breaking this goal (also known as an 'epic') into sprints, and continuously seeking and acting on feedback in each sprint. If you had four sprints and four business units, each sprint might involve extending the rollout to a unique business unit. At the end of each sprint, you would reflect on what you and the team had learned and what you could then take forward and change in your approach in the next sprint. This approach would therefore be *iterative* in nature: dynamic, and acting on new information as it comes in, all with the aim of being better and better as you move towards the end goal.

Embracing multidisciplinarity

In the original *Manifesto for Agile Software Development*, the authors stress how 'business people and developers must work together daily throughout the project'.[2] Experiences have subsequently shown that there is even greater value if a plurality of skills and viewpoints are held within digital teams. In Chapter 16 we explore further the specific roles and skills that digital teams should have, but broadly speaking, a great multidisciplinary team, working on a given 'epic', should have a:

- *product/service owner/manager:* usually this is the notional team leader and the interface with the wider parts of the business;
- *delivery manager:* this individual is focused on removing any obstacles that are preventing team members from doing their jobs, and sets up and runs key meetings;
- *business analyst (may be more than one):* responsible for defining, generating and conducting business analysis or data science;
- *user researcher (may be more than one):* conducts research with users to uncover their needs, and tests digital solutions with them;
- *service designer:* identifies issues with current digital services or proposes improvements;
- *technical architect:* maps, defines and proposes new and future technical architectures to ensure fully functioning digital services and seamless data flows;
- *software engineer/developer:* designs, builds, runs and maintains digital services;
- *data scientist:* seeks out opportunities for optimizing services through use of data, and applies this where relevant.

Not all projects will need all of these roles full-time. Some may require additional roles and some individuals may be able to fulfil more than one role concurrently, but broadly speaking, these are the key roles required. In addition to these disciplines, it is important that individuals who have experience *across* the areas of the business you are working in are part of the team. This will avoid siloed thinking.

Encouraging equality of thought and input

Related to the multidisciplinary point, agile teams work in relatively flat and low bureaucracy structures. This means there is little in the way of 'management overhead'. Each team member should be focused on delivering the team's agreed end goal, not generating internal reports. Team members should feel empowered and collectively accountable for delivery of the team's objectives. In key meetings, all team members should be treated as equals, free to contribute to problem-solving and raise concerns, unencumbered by fears of speaking out of place. While the product owner may ultimately have responsibility for the running of the product or service, it is their role to facilitate debate and bring together opposing views.

Working in the open

Agile teams work in uncertain environments. As such, it is especially important for them to communicate frequently and transparently to peers, stakeholders and, if appropriate, even customers and the outside world. Communications should cover what they are doing, how they are progressing, and challenges they are encountering. For example, Facebook runs a 'Facebook for Developers' community with blogs, frequently asked questions pages, newsletters, videos and more to explain what they are working on.

While you have a wide variety of channels to choose from – social media, podcasts, newsletters, vlogs, etc – at bare minimum it's advisable to work in the open in at least three ways:

1 *Prioritize 'showing the thing'.* At every opportunity, demonstrate the technology you are working on to stakeholders. Don't hide it away until it's 'ready'. Instead, use outward communications as an opportunity to test and refine.

2 *Run 'show and tell' sessions internally.* At the end of each sprint, run a 30-minute or one-hour meeting that is open to all interested stakeholders in your organization. In this meeting, talk about what you've worked on in this sprint, the progress you've made, any challenges you've encountered,

and what's coming up next. This openness will win you allies, gain excitement and should reduce the need for other reporting requirements.

3 **Write about your progress.** This can be for an internal *and* an external audience, if appropriate (if you're working on something in security, or highly competitive, this may be less wise). Often this can take the form of blogs or end-of-week missives called 'week notes'; the content and style should be accessible and informal. You're writing for multiple reasons: to excite people about your work; to reach out for help or ideas; and to invite comment and feedback. Lots of examples are about, but the Canadian Digital Service blog is a good place to get a sense of what this could look like.[3]

Fulfilling the 'rituals'

'Rituals' is a fancy agile word for sensible team meetings. They are also known sometimes as 'ceremonies'. The key meetings you should immediately stick in the calendar are: *daily stand-ups* – the whole team should attend, and in less than 15 minutes everyone should say what they did yesterday, what they're doing today, and anything that's blocking their progress; *sprint retrospectives* – at the end of sprint, the team should get together to review what worked well and what worked less well; and *sprint planning* – conversely, at the start of a sprint, the team should also get together to plan the work ahead.

Choosing – and sticking to – a project management approach that works for you

There are various agile software management approaches you can choose from. Confluence, Asana, Monday, Jira and Trello are all highly recom-

FIGURE 4.1 An example Kanban board for a sprint

Epic	To do	Doing	Done
Understand our user needs	...	...	...
Establish service blueprint	...		
Develop future models			

mended, although fundamentally, you can do what they do using a pen and some Post-Its. This approach is also known as a 'scrum' approach, and key elements of it include:

- Using *Kanban boards* during sprints: this involves a table with three columns (see Figure 4.1). The first column contains 'tasks to do'; the second column has 'tasks in progress'; and the final column (unsurprisingly) is where 'completed' tasks lie. Each task should have an owner, an estimated time to undertake, and a completion date. All of these tasks form your *backlog*. Make sure to use the Kanban during your *stand-ups*.
- *Backlog grooming.* Every week, go through the backlog and check what is still open, relevant and if anything is missing. Add or amend as appropriate.
- *Burndown charts.* Each team member will have a finite number of hours they can work on during a sprint. Each task will take a defined amount of time. With these figures you can work out if you have enough resources to complete your tasks. If you do, great; if you don't, reprioritize the Kanban.

The most important point, however, is to use the tools that work for you and use them consistently. Not every tool works in every scenario, so use your retrospectives to consider what's working and what needs changing, and act accordingly.

Where next?

So how do you mobilize and get your digital transformation started? First, based on your roadmap, determine how many projects and workstreams you are going to tackle at any one time. From this you'll know how many teams you need. Then you need to *get the team in place*. This is no mean feat – you need the right skills, experience and capabilities. Chapter 16 covers where you might find these individuals or how you might train up existing staff, but either way, your team will make your efforts a success or failure.

You also need to make sure you have *sufficient resourcing*. Are your team members dedicated, full-time on the work, or part-time? Are there constraints on their availability? Once you know your backlog, sense-check whether you have enough resources in place. If not, you'll have to reprioritize the backlog so resources match demand.

Move on quickly to *setting up the team rituals*. The team delivery manager is probably the best person to do this. Get the stand-ups, retrospectives, show-and-tells and sprint planning in the diary. In your first sprint planning session, create the backlog for the sprint and get cracking!

BRINGING THE PRINCIPLE TO LIFE
Agile ways of working in global care home chain

Where can we look for an agile, flexible, progressive organization? Silicon Valley? Financial services? Artificial intelligence start-ups?

How about a Dutch nursing home? Founded in 2006, Buurtzorg is a chain of care homes across the Netherlands with over 10,000 staff. Rather than adopt traditional business models, such as corporate functions, business units and regional centres, Buurtzorg eschewed these for a community-based, team approach. Though the founder of Buurtzorg, Jos de Blok, did not explicitly set out to create an agile culture, the principles the company holds dear, particularly empowered, autonomous teams, are agile to the core. The model involves self-managed teams of no more than 12 nurses serving a community of approximately 5,000 people. A small number of constraints are set – such as caps on office rent or furniture costs – and lean corporate functions support the teams, but ultimately the teams are responsible and accountable for the care they deliver.

The outcomes? Two evaluations, one by EY and another by KPMG, both found that the Buurtzorg model of care reduced hospital admissions, improved patient outcomes, and led to lower costs than other sector providers.[4] Staff experience was also found to be exceptional: between 2010 and 2016, Buurtzorg was named Dutch Employer of the Year five times. The model is now operational in over 25 countries.[5]

Buurtzorg is particularly important because it demonstrates how agile approaches need not be solely confined to software-heavy organizations. Caring for vulnerable or older individuals is as important a job as there is, though this is not a sector you would immediately associate with technological advancement. Yet the great agile disciplines of empowered teams, flexible working and best use of technology to manage workloads have all shown to be applicable at Buurtzorg. One of the biggest fears senior executives have for adopting agile ways of working is a concern that transparency will reduce, reporting information will be minimized and, should something go wrong, it will be harder to understand why. Yet the care sector is highly regulated and agile has been proven to be effective here. If it can work here, it can surely work in your organization too.

Tips and tricks

- Agile is about making operations better. Its techniques are just a means to an end, not an end in themselves.
- Facing agile sceptics in your organization? Point them to the problems that agile ways of working are trying to solve. If your sceptics recognize these problems in your organization – and usually, if they exist, they are pretty hard to dispute – reassure them that agile is all about specifically addressing these problems.
- There are lots of software options available to help run agile approaches – pick one carefully and try to stick to it.
- If you can prioritize just one aspect of agile, make it user-centred design. By truly understanding who your users are and what they need from you, you'll be able to focus all your efforts solely on delighting your users.
- If you prioritize just two aspects, make the second one empowering teams. Great teams do great things.

What you might say in your next meeting

Agile means focusing exclusively on what matters to our customers.

Agile might have been born out of software development, but its principles are applicable everywhere.

Let's not be too precious about the methodology. What matters is that it works for us.

Agile doesn't mean we don't have to report on progress, just that we should only make reports that are actually valuable to people in our organization or wider stakeholders.

Let's try and join as many 'show and tells' as we can – it'll show our colleagues that we're serious about these new ways of working.

Where you can find out more

For an excellent introduction to the ethos and techniques underpinning agile, try Neil Perkin's *Agile Transformation: Structures, processes and mindsets for the digital age* (Kogan Page, 2019).

Notes

1 Beck, K, *et al* (2001) *Manifesto for Agile Software Development*, Agile Alliance, Corryton, TN

2 Beck, K, *et al* (2001) *Manifesto for Agile Software Development*, Agile Alliance, Corryton, TN

3 Canadian Digital Service blog, digital.canada.ca/blog/index.html (archived at https://perma.cc/Q7G4-LCKK)

4 Johansen, F and Van den Bosch, S (2017) The scaling-up of Neighbourhood Care: From experiment towards a transformative movement in healthcare, *Futures*, **89**

5 For more on the Buurtzorg model, see Prabhu, J (2021) *How Should a Government Be?* Profile Books, London

05

Senior and organizational buy-in

Digital transformation will impact the whole of the organization. How can you make sure you have the support you need?

The principle in a nutshell

In John Kotter's seminal guide to transformation, *Our Iceberg is Melting*, the second stage of the eight-stage process for change management is simply put as 'create a guiding coalition'.[1] There is much to commend this point. Subsequent reviews of transformation failures commonly point to a lack of leadership and organizational buy-in and support as a critical factor in the failure.[2] For your digital transformation to succeed, it's vital to get support at *all levels* and *throughout* the organization. *At all levels*, because senior leadership is vital, but so is support from front-line staff. And *throughout* is essential because otherwise support and interest will become siloed. This might be OK at the start – but as your work impacts on wider parts of the business, the lack of support will cause you problems. If your digital transformation is described as an 'IT thing' or people say 'that's for the digital team', you should be worried. Successful buy-in means support extends beyond the domains of technology.

Buy-in is easy to say but hard to achieve. You cannot – usually – mandate someone to support you. You need to consider staff needs, motivations and concerns. Adroitness and sensitivity are required to win over sceptics. It's hard work, but if you don't do it, your chances of success will plummet.

What's the problem being addressed?

Getting organizational buy-in is not a 'nice to have'. It is utterly essential to the success of your endeavours. How do you deal with that irascible executive director who always says, 'I just don't get technology – it's not my thing'? The easiest thing is to ignore them. But that risks a whole heap of problems further down the line. Facing up to the challenges head on will help in:

- *Getting senior support:* even the flattest of organizations have a degree of hierarchy. Ultimately, if the most senior and accountable individuals are against your digital transformation, it's almost impossible to succeed. When you hit a wall, when delivery slows down, or when you need more money, you will need seniors in the organization to step in and support you.

- *Making it everyone's problem:* good digital transformation breaks down organizational silos. That means you need to work *across* all parts of the business to change things from end-to-end. Inevitably, this means the transformation will depend on people and parts of the enterprise far removed from classic digital or technology department structures. So you need to prime those parts of the business; get them excited, wanting and wishing to see you succeed, because they will benefit from the success as well.

- *Knowing who's a sceptic:* part of the process of getting buy-in is diagnostic. You need to know who's with you and who's against you. And you also need to appreciate that this may be dynamic and due to various factors. Identifying your supporters and sceptics and having a clear approach for working with each – all the basics of good stakeholder engagement and management – will put you in good stead in your digital efforts.

Putting the principle into action

Getting support and buy-in requires a multi-pronged approach, patience and sometimes a bit of luck. But most importantly, it requires you to do a good job. The best way to get buy-in is to evidence that you are actually delivering what you said you would do. No amount of bluffing can hide failure forever. But the following approaches will complement successful delivery.

Get to know your stakeholders

Who's important to your digital transformation? If you're implementing a new enterprise software solution, don't kid yourself that the IT director is the only person you need to worry about – the clue is in the name *enterprise*: you need support from all senior stakeholders. Similarly, if you're trying to roll out a new decision-making tool for healthcare clinicians, the chief medical officer in the hospital might love the product, but if the finance director doesn't want to pay for it, you've got a problem. So think laterally and carefully about who's involved. How would you categorize these individuals? Think along classic lines: who's accountable; who's responsible for delivery (possibly you); who needs to be consulted about changes; and who needs to be kept informed?

Run an exercise to map out each of these stakeholders. You can do this individually or as a team. Revisit the map regularly. Hatch a plan for how you will treat each of your differing stakeholder groups and stick to it.

Pick your champions

A slide deck explaining why people should care about the work you're doing won't change anything. Nor will an impressive model claiming lots of financial benefits. People are what get people excited about change. So think carefully: who is going to change your work in the organization? Who is going to join an 'all staff' meeting and herald the benefits of what you're doing? Who's going to have your back when things go wrong? You need to have a few, well-chosen champions to support your efforts.

What does a great champion look like? This will depend on your organization and what you're trying to do. But it's wise to have a mix of senior staff from varying parts of the organization. Moving your corporate data from internal servers to the cloud certainly needs your chief technology officer to be the lead champion, but having some front-line staff who can clearly articulate why this matters – ideally how it will make their lives and the lives of their colleagues better – will be even more powerful because it's unexpected.

Create the right conditions

In order to effect change you need to ensure multiple motivations and incentives are being addressed. The equilibrium incentivization model (Figure 5.1) provides a helpful framework for considering what levers you can pull.[3]

FIGURE 5.1 Equilibrium incentivization model

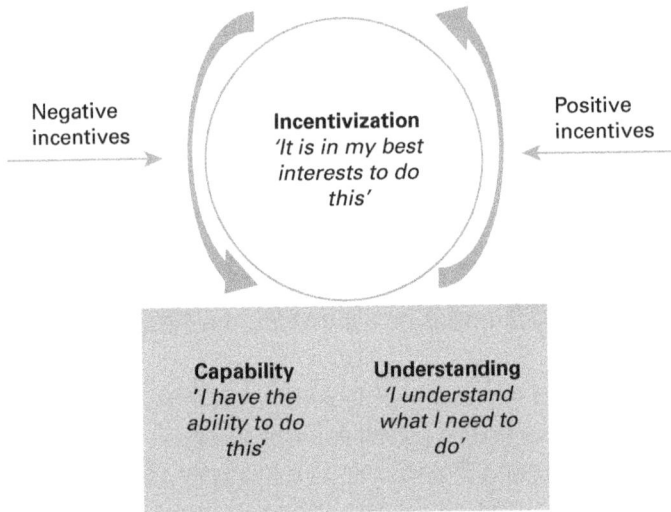

From an individual and organization perspective, you want people to be *positively incentivized* to embrace your digital transformation. This can take a number of guises: suppliers could be financially rewarded for compliance with new data regulations; individuals seeing their seniors supporting the digital transformation should be able to see how this might help their career prospects; and simple, gamified approaches can spur motivation, such as measuring which teams are the first to successfully migrate onto new platforms. The PSC, a digital consultancy, runs transformation programmes in a way that invites secondments from 'high potential individuals' to bid to lead workstreams, providing them with a way to learn new skills and progress in their organization.

On the flip side, *negative incentives* can also help staff realize that 'it is in my best interests' to support the transformation. These can include fines for non-compliance, or explicit performance management of individuals or business units that are behind on their plans. Most famously, Amazon CEO Jeff Bezos announced in 2002 that all teams had to share their data with other teams via APIs (application program interfaces). So if finance wanted some HR data on staff members, HR couldn't just email over the information – they would have to define their data and make it available to be accessed via an API. Bezos finished his edict with the ultimate negative incentive, the line: 'Anyone who doesn't do this will be fired. Thank you; have a nice day!'[4]

It's also critical to *develop the capabilities* necessary to deliver the transformation. It was possible for Bezos to mandate APIs because each team in Amazon had software engineers and developers with the necessary capabilities to define, develop and maintain APIs for anyone to access. That won't be the case in many organizations. There are two ways to develop capabilities: bringing new people in (either permanently or temporarily) or upskilling and training existing staff. The first can be expensive and disruptive, the latter disruptive and time-consuming. But this is the reality of transformation. It is also why it's so important to define very clearly what you need from teams within the organization. If you need the analytics team to move to a cloud-based analytics provider so you can access data in a trusted research environment (one where sensitive data doesn't leave a validated, verified host organization; it's all accessed remotely via secure connections), upskilling staff in PowerBI, for instance, probably isn't too challenging. However, if you are woolly in your requirements, such as by saying 'we need better analytics', it's unreasonable to expect staff with no experience in this area to know what to do. Instead, you'll be likely to require external resources.

And last but by no means least, it's vital that your staff have a *clear understanding* of why they are being asked to support new ways of working. Without this, at best they will do the bare minimum required of them. But if they understand the rationale, this can help to gain support, motivation and potentially spur innovation as individuals think of new and better ways to meet the brief. At Shopify, the ecommerce platform, staff are invited to 'Ask Me Anything' (known as 'AMA' and popularized by the chat forum Reddit) sessions where they are encouraged to grill their seniors on everything: strategy; sustainability; and even pay and conditions are all discussed at AMA meetings. Such sessions provide an open forum for debate and encourage discussions that provide an excellent opportunity to frankly express why your digital strategy needs to be enacted. If your CEO is uncertain, you might be able to convince them by pointing out that US President Obama ran an AMA session on Reddit in 2012.

Show the thing

Relating back to the ways of working we covered in Chapter 4, show-and-tells are a hugely powerful way to get organizational buy-in. Digital isn't really about concepts or theories or strategies. It's about products and services that make people's lives better. And so there's no better way of proving that reality (or at least possibility) than showing how you're working towards making things better. Choose your invite list for show-and-tells wisely – you want a wide audience, ideally as wide as possible, but don't spring any unwelcome surprises on people (like: 'here's how our robotic process automation can reduce our need for the finance team... oh, hello finance team'). So lay the groundwork beforehand if you need to. But ultimately, always err on the side of transparency in how you work.

Where next?

Buy-in isn't static. So keep on revisiting these approaches throughout the transformation and throughout your delivery of the roadmap. Your first step should be to use your roadmap to help you understand all the stakeholders who are relevant to its different components. Develop a plan for engagement for stakeholders. Book time in their diaries. Cultivate your champions and make them know how important they are to the work. Make one of your team members accountable for keeping an eye on progress. And, very importantly, book in your show-and-tells and invite people to join.

You will face bumps and challenges along the road. But the best thing you can do to overcome scepticism is proof of delivery. So if you're facing delays or cost overruns, point out how you're still significantly on track to deliver your roadmap. If senior stakeholders move and change, as they often do, don't assume that someone new in post will support you like their predecessor did. You need to start the buy-in process again and win them over. It's relentless. But utterly necessary.

BRINGING THE PRINCIPLE TO LIFE
Moving to a service design culture from the top in a major government department

The UK Department for Education had historically been mainly known for producing policy for governing early years provision, schools and colleges across England. Over a decade of reforms during the 2010s, its requirements changed significantly – as schools and colleges gained more autonomy, the need grew for the department to be less policy-oriented and more focused on delivering services – such as funding, special support, access to technology, teacher recruitment and so forth for education institutions. All of these services *could* have a strong digital element, with the services effectively being end-to-end digital offerings, rather than paper or physical processes. And yet despite these changing requirements, up until the mid-2010s, the department had changed relatively little in its operations.

Around 2017, the departmental permanent secretary announced that it needed to 'move from being a department known for producing policy, to one of end-to-end, continuous policy and delivery' – effectively an end-to-end service model, with digital at the heart of everything it did. This was a significant change and met with some cultural resistance. Yet a small team in the department set about to change minds and win over hearts. The transformation embraced agile ways of working. Show-and-tells were set up to demonstrate progress. Support was championed at the very top, by the head of the department, the permanent secretary. Individuals were positively incentivized by encouraging them to join cross-cutting 'service teams' built around specific end-to-end user needs, with these teams celebrated in the department. New capabilities were established, including a user-centred design lab, to truly understand the needs of the many users the department catered for. Champions were sought throughout the organization, with new 'service owners' typically being former deputy directors (one of the most senior levels in the organization).

It was by no means plain sailing, but after three years the department could reflect on some huge achievements. By 2020, the transformation team had grown from four individuals in a single location to over 120, in three sites across the country. And 22 new digital services were up and running, offering simplified, end-to-end services to teachers, educational administrators and parents across the country – with 12 more services in the pipeline.[5]

Tips and tricks

- Know your enemy. Unless you have a sense of what people truly think about what you're trying to do, you won't know if you have a problem or not.

- Don't hide behind your friends and supporters. You need to win over the sceptics too.

- Choose more than just the 'likely suspects' to be your digital champions. They don't need to be senior; they just need to be respected in the organization.

- Treat support as something very dynamic. Individuals are free to change their minds and so you shouldn't take anyone's support for granted.

- Above all else, focus on doing a good job. That's the best way to get people to support you.

What you might say in your next meeting

Let's map out everyone who's relevant to our digital roadmap.

When are we next speaking to all of these individuals?

Who came to the last show-and-tell? And more importantly, who *didn't*?

What feedback are we hearing about our work? Do we need to be worried?

We have so many supporters out there. We need to be smart about how we make the most of their goodwill.

Where you can find out more

We started the chapter talking about John Kotter's *Leading Change*. Written with Holger Rathgeber, *Our Iceberg is Melting: Changing and succeeding under any conditions* (Macmillan, 2006) is an even more accessible – and highly enjoyable – must-read primer for the fundamentals of good transformation. Remember, digital transformation is still transformation.

Notes

1 Kotter, J (1995) *Leading Change*, Harvard Business Review Press, Boston
2 Bartsch, S, *et al* (2020) Leadership matters in crisis-induced digital transformation: how to lead service employees effectively during the COVID-19 pandemic, *Journal of Service Management*, 32(1), doi/10.1108/JOSM-05-2020-0160/
3 Weiss, A (2011) *Key Business Solutions: Essential problem-solving tools and techniques that every manager needs to know*, Pearson, Cambridge
4 Kim, J (2017) The API manifesto success story, *ProFocus Technology*, 22 November, www.profocustechnology.com/enterprise/api-manifesto-success-story/ (archived at https://perma.cc/U87H-6MKD)
5 Stace, E (2020) *DfE Digital – Looking back three years on*, dfedigital.blog.gov.uk/2020/05/01/emma-stace-3-years/ (archived at https://perma.cc/KN77-98FM)

06

Funding digital

In many ways, it really is all about the money. So whether you like it or not, accept or embrace this and work out who's going to pay for your digital transformation agenda, and how.

The principle in a nutshell

Digital transformation seems to operate in two very separate worlds. One world is that of the business news and mainstream media – where Tesla, Facebook, Amazon, Apple, Netflix and Google dominate the popular imagination, where billion-dollar start-up valuations are the norm and money is no impediment to famous tech entrepreneurs, where the fact that it took Amazon nine years to make a profit, incurring billions of dollars of losses along the way, is written off as 'just the way things are'.

The other world is probably the one you inhabit – where upgrading essential hardware like PCs and devices is a fight with the finance department, where the board will only sign off on the digital transformation plans if they promise to deliver huge financial savings, where you definitely *do not* have the luxury of nearly a decade to make huge losses before finally breaking even. In this world, finance is king, and nothing happens without the pounds and dollars being carefully tracked and monitored. The watchful eye of finance is a necessary evil. And there are better and worse ways of doing it: too much oversight and you stifle innovation; too little, and you risk an expensive free-for-all.

What's the problem being addressed?

Getting the right balance in funding digital is far from easy. Numerous competing pressures need to be balanced when doing so:

- *Funding enough to ensure delivery:* penny-pinching in digital transformation is never wise. The trade-off between cost and quality is a false one: do it well and properly and you won't have to do it twice. Your funding envelope needs to cover your digital transformation plans. To do that, of course, requires you to know how much funding you need.

- *And funding enough to allow mistakes:* innovation and new ways of doing things are at the heart of digital transformation. And with this comes inevitable mistakes and missteps. You cannot know everything in advance. With new digital services, you may discover unanticipated user needs that require additional development. Or actual mistakes may occur during implementation, picked up during error testing (called 'debugging'), which require rework. Either way, your funding needs to give enough slack to allow for this.

- *Giving confidence that benefits will be realized:* you should expect improvements from your transformation. If they are not delivered, stakeholders will rightly interrogate whether money was wasted. Smart financing of digital should be able to get the balance right. Piloting, or rolling out changes step by step, should give enough information to know whether something is on track or not, and thus whether more funding should follow.

- *Breaking down barriers:* false economies need to be watched out for. Reducing costs in one team – maybe customer services – might lead to new costs in another – potentially compliance, for instance. Your funding arrangements need to reflect that great digital transformation happens across an organization, not within silos.

- *Minimizing bureaucracy:* releasing funds and tracking progress carries its own business costs. Your funding approach needs to be lightweight enough to not distract expensive digital teams from their core job, but robust enough to make sure money is being spent wisely.

Putting the principle into action

Financing digital transformation is a complex and ongoing process. You can't just assume that because your roadmap has senior support that it will be financed appropriately.

Who's paying and how?

First, you need to know how transformation gets paid for in your enterprise. Usually it's either via a central transformation fund pot, which sits outside of business units or departments, or the transformation funding needs to come from the units themselves. The latter approach risks creating silos: one department's plans may lead to cost pressures elsewhere, which get missed in the financing process. The former approach can result in a bidding war. It's highly unlikely that your digital plans will be the only bidders for the coveted transformation funds. As such, it's important that you can clearly articulate what you are aiming to do, why, and then you can quantify – insofar as is possible or sensible – the costs and benefits of your ambitions. This usually takes the form of a *business case*.

When funding happens and how money gets released will also vary in organizations. Table 6.1 outlines the three most typical ways. A *business as usual* approach treats transformation as nothing special – effectively a department or business unit just makes a request in the budgeting process for any new technology adoption. For example, if the legal team wants to improve how cases are handled in the organization, they might request monies to purchase, implement and pay licence fees and any ongoing costs for a new case management system. The legal team would then make a bid to the finance team that runs the budgeting process, setting out the in-year costs (remember costs may take place over more than one year) and the monies would either be approved or not.

The next two approaches both involve *business cases*. A business case can serve multiple purposes, but ultimately it should be a document that sets out a strategic direction, lays out one or more options for achieving that direction, and then quantifies – by assessing the costs and benefits of each option – which is the best option. The business case should then explain how much the preferred option will cost, over what timeframe, and set out a plan for implementing the option. In a business case where an organization is looking to make it easier to manage and publish the content it shares with its customers, the case would most likely look at a number of options for content management system technologies and set out the case for a preferred technology.

Once an option is agreed via appropriate governance structures – this should involve ensuring senior stakeholders support the business case, and that finance teams are sighted on the cost implications – the main remaining question is *when* to release the monies. A *stage-gate* approach results in releasing tranches of funding, dependent on milestones being hit. These can helpfully be tied to your digital roadmap. For instance, in Chapter 9 we discuss the importance of breaking up the project lifecycle into discovery, alpha, beta and live phases. Each of these phases could act as a milestone at which – providing certain progress could be demonstrated – monies could be released.

An *all-in-one* approach, conversely, means that as soon as funding is approved, it is released directly to the teams. Usually in seed investment – early stage – financing of start-ups, this is the approach taken. It has the benefit of minimizing hoops that teams have to jump through to prove progress. However, it also can mean that there is little transparency on how money is being spent. If this approach is taken, the importance of working in the open (as covered in Chapter 4) is even more critical to mitigate any concerns about a lack of transparency around delivery of the transformation.

Working out how much to fund

The most critical part of funding digital is knowing how much is required. While you can be relatively confident about costs in the short term – but even then, events like a cyber attack or unanticipated service outage can rapidly skew costs – if you are planning for more than a year out, uncertainty abounds.

When thinking about the *cost side*, the following considerations should be at the front of mind.

Who is delivering the *overall transformation costs*? This should include people costs (eg, head of digital transformation), contractor or agency costs

TABLE 6.1 Summary of different funding approaches for digital transformation

Funding approach	Business as usual	Business case with stage-gate	Business case with 'all in one'
Usually delivered by	In the budget-setting process, by department budget	By special business case, in the budget-setting process	By special business case, in the budget-setting process
Pros	Lightweight, minimal senior input	Provides opportunities to check on progress	Minimizes bureaucracy
Cons	Very little scrutiny, potentially invites bias	Can be bureaucratic	Risk that if something goes wrong, no opportunity to correct

(such as consultancy advice) and the inevitable costs involved in governance (for example, generating reports, attending meetings, briefing senior stakeholders). Are these new costs or people doing work 'side of desk'? If the latter, do you need to quantify the opportunity cost of their time? The simplest way to do this is to estimate the time they will spend on the transformation as a proportion of their working year, and multiply their annual salary by this. It's important that when you compare options in your business case, you use common assumptions, such as whether or not to quantify 'side of desk' time, throughout.

For each different digital development you are undertaking, you will also need to consider:

- What goes into *development and implementation costs*? This will usually either be the cost of digital teams – developers, software engineers, technical architects and so on – building a new service over a given period of time. Or it will be the cost of technical teams implementing software or rolling out hardware. To work out these costs, you will need to use a combination of: asking other teams or organizations who've implemented something similar; getting multiple quotes from suppliers; estimating costs of technical teams; and calculating how long implementation will take.

- How much will *running costs* be, and over what timeframe? It's vital to remember that once a digital product or technology is implemented or built, it still needs to be run. These costs can break down into operational costs: such as costs of hosting, licences for users, business continuity testing to ensure the technology is stable, and helpdesks for users encountering difficulties with the technology. In addition, there are likely to be continuous improvement costs, such as upgrades or maintenance costs or patching to fix security concerns. A lot of these costs are 'variable' – they will increase with volume of usage (usually the number of users), whereas development and implementation costs are typically 'fixed'. If you are onboarding a supplier, you need to fully understand what all of these costs are, which costs are covered by one-off implementation costs, and how variable costs might change over time. One of the challenges with buying any licensed goods is that you are likely to be required to pay for licences for the lifespan of the products or service. You need to factor this into your total cost calculations.

For all costs, you should consider applying *optimism bias*. This is based on the behavioural science observation that humans invariably underestimate how long a change will take or cost. Optimism bias will vary depending on how far away you are from actually undertaking the digital transformation, but a range of 20–200 per cent is not imprudent. If you have a high degree of confidence in your cost figures and are very close to starting the transformation, a lower figure is appropriate. If you're in the opposite scenario, the inverse applies.

A final cost question, which is usually one more for the accountants than the digital teams, is nonetheless important, and that's whether costs count as a *capital* or *revenue* cost in the organizational financial ledger. This mainly matters because, for many organizations, it's easier to borrow money or fund digital projects if they are treated as 'capital': that is, an asset that adds value to the business. This cost is depreciated and amortized – effectively spread out over time – in a way that revenue costs are not. So, it's worth a conversation with your finance teams: what are the implications of capital and revenue financing for funding my digital transformation?

When thinking about the *benefits side* it's important not to get too caught up in a 'how much money is this going to save us?' conversation. Digitization in many instances *should* save money, particularly when the end-to-end transformation means that previously highly labour-intensive tasks (such as call centres or physical advice kiosks) can be partially replaced by automated, digital services such as chatbots. However, in many instances, digitization may actually *increase* costs. You might uncover new user needs that need fulfilling. New technologies might require a minimum number of users before they are actually cheaper to run than what they replaced. Or sometimes you have to 'double-run' services. 'Double-running' is particularly common in government services, whereby many services are universal, which means they have to be accessible to everyone. Because not everyone is comfortable or able to use digital services (this is a term sometimes called 'digital literacy'), it's likely that non-digital options must still be in place too alongside the digital offering.

That said, it's inevitable you will be asked to consider what types of benefits your new technologies might cover. These usually include:

- *Cashable or cash-releasing benefits:* this is where the new technology has freed up expenditure that may no longer be needed. For example, moving to a cloud-based analytics platform might reduce costs in two ways: it might free up server costs for data storage, and it might reduce the number of staff required to undertake analysis. Cashable benefits are mainly found in headcount numbers, because so much of organizational costs are due to staffing costs, so if you are looking for benefits in these areas consider how your digital transformation might change the shape and size of teams in your organization. Not all efficiencies need to be cashable, mind. If you can release staff time to be used on other, more productive activities, you are also delivering a benefit.

- *Avoided costs:* other types of quantifiable benefit include where digital transformation helps reduce expenditure in the future. This could be because: you no longer need to maintain or run a particular piece of technology; the new technology enables you to buy less of something, or buy it at a cheaper price; or the new technology minimizes compliance or fines or penalties.

- *Increased revenue:* new technologies – particularly related to fields of ecommerce and digital marketing – may also facilitate increasing income. Here it's important to consider how to compare options against each other. If you run an online business, the choice won't be between no online revenue and some; it will be between different platforms and services that allow you to generate revenues.

- *Enabling benefits:* sometimes a change is essential to your wider transformation, but it's hard to put a cash figure on the direct benefits arising. This is usually because it's an enabling benefit: it allows something else to happen that has its own benefits. Moving your data to a cloud platform is a classic enabler; this should enable lots of different products or services and their attendant benefits to run from the cloud. When creating your benefits case, it's worth being explicit about enabling benefits so stakeholders can see the value of something, even if it's not explicitly quantifiable.

- *Innovation benefits:* slightly more conceptual, innovation benefits come from the belief that investing in certain things – research and development being the most obvious example – will lead to new innovations further down the line. This is an important point, and often in hindsight becomes the thing people truly value from a change – who'd have thought videoconferencing technology would enable so much of the economy to function during Covid-19, for instance? Again, in a business case, it's worth just articulating how you think innovation *might* arise from your proposed investments.

Governance and tracking delivery

Particularly if funding is enabled via a 'business case with stage-gates' route, good governance is vital. Tomes have been written on what good governance entails, yet it remains a much-contested business topic. Ideally, a minimum viable approach to good governance for digital business cases would be one where there is an investment/finance board that oversees and grants business case funding requests. Such a board would also track progress and delivery of the plans and roadmaps set out in the business cases on a regular basis.

If funding has been granted via a 'business as usual' approach, it's none-theless important to make a clear note of what was funded, when and for what purposes. An investment board could still track business case delivery even if funding is released in an 'all in one go' format.

The ideal composition of the investment board will vary from organiza-tion to organization, but it should at least have a sufficiently senior representative from finance to have the authority to grant funding. And each business case, and associated digital delivery initiative, should have an indi-vidual who is ultimately accountable for the delivery of the initiative, of whom questions can be asked at the investment board if delivery is off track.

It is important to provide the investment board with the necessary data on which decisions can be made and delivery tracked. Often less is more, particularly if many initiatives are being considered, and so it's helpful to think about what are the fewest, most valuable sets of indicators that can help to give a sense of delivery. You should consider:

- *Lagging indicators:* these will most likely be the benefits that your business case articulated. Have they been delivered in the timescales envisaged?

- *Leading indicators:* these can be extremely useful in giving a sense of whether your lagging indicators are likely to be realized. For example, if your digital initiative is to roll out a new level of cyber-security accredita-tion across the organization, your lagging indicators might include avoided costs from fines or penalties, but your *leading indicators* could be the number of teams or business units that have successfully been accredited. By tracking these indicators, you should have a good sense of progress.

Where next?

Your digital roadmap should set the foundations for all funding considera-tions. Start the simple conversation with your senior stakeholders and finance colleagues: how are we going to pay for this? That should then guide you as to what type of business case you may need to develop, what data you need to track, and how money will be released to your team.

Many digital leaders consider that business cases and financial considerations are a distraction from their core job of transforming working practices through technology. While this is understandable, it betrays a negative mindset that will be self-perpetuating. Embrace the questions and scrutiny from finance colleagues. Ultimately, they are trying to ensure that money is being spent well and wisely. It's hard to begrudge that.

Once you have your approvals for spending, don't take your eyes off the requirements you may have to report on progress and remember that you should be aiming to deliver the benefits you identified in your business case. That said, business cases are not the same thing as actual delivery – as you develop your technologies, you may uncover that certain benefits will not be delivered, while others might. You need to transparently update your stakeholders on these findings as you go, and change what you report on for progress as necessary. To paraphrase the economist John Maynard Keynes, when the facts change, you must change your plans too.

BRINGING THE PRINCIPLE TO LIFE
Enabling cross-department collaboration through funding digital projects

Since 1833, in the United Kingdom public finances have been closely watched over by one of the smallest government departments: the Treasury. Set up amid a background of concerns around national debt arising from the 17th-century South Sea Bubble, which precipitated an economic crisis, since its foundation the Treasury has fiercely interrogated public expenditure on what was known as a 'bilateral' basis. Government departments and public bodies would each submit financial plans to the Treasury, which would be subsequently scrutinized, and if deemed necessary, reduced.

While this approach has been lauded and replicated across the world, it presents a very clear risk of creating silos. Under this model, it would not be in, say, the business department's financial interests to invest in a new technology that benefited any other department: each department would look out for themselves only. In order to overcome this challenge, in 2019 the UK government announced the creation of a £200 million 'Shared Outcomes Fund' pilot. This allowed multiple government departments to jointly bid for funding to undertake transformations that would benefit more than just a single department.

In one of the largest bids, nearly £10 million was split between seven government departments for a data improvement project that sought to 'improve the cross-departmental evidence base and use of data to inform policy decisions and service delivery for children and young people'. Akin to the stage-gate business model described earlier, the seven departments presented a joint business case to the Treasury, which was approved, and subsequently jointly reported on progress against the case at regular milestones. This requires departments to work together towards jointly shared outcomes and deliverables, reducing the silo mentality and demonstrating how even the oldest of institutions can innovate. With 24 pilots funded initially, the Shared Outcomes Fund was subsequently rolled out even further, with another £200 million made available for a second round of funding.[1]

Tips and tricks

- Technology needs to be paid for, so familiarize yourselves with the financial environment you are operating in. Will you be expected to facilitate significant savings? How much grace will you be given if things don't go quite to plan?

- What's your relationship like with finance colleagues? Does your organization have finance business partners who shadow departments, or do you need to reach out to build connections in finance? Like any request for money, it's best not to come cold.

- Focus on the costs more than the benefits when quantifying your digital transformation. Benefits are important, but anyone can multiply numbers together to get an attractive answer. Be wary of banking too much on projected benefits. Costs will ultimately be cash going out of the business and need to be as accurate as possible.

- When developing your optimism bias percentage uplift, look back on previous digital projects in your organization and try and get a sense of how close they were to hitting their expected costs. Can this be used as a good basis for an optimism bias uplift figure?

- Track and monitor delivery of your digital initiative carefully. Use this monitoring as a feedback loop. If you're on a good trajectory, great, but if not, what do you need to change to correct things?

What you might say in your next meeting

We've got our vision, but how are we going to pay for it?

I'd rather be pessimistic and prudent with our costings than the other way around.

Let's use the process of funding our projects as an opportunity to improve our plans, rather than view it as a hindrance.

It doesn't matter if finance isn't interested in how we're spending the money – we should always be interested in this.

Tracking our delivery against anticipated benefits will help us know if things are going well or not.

Where you can find out more

For all the ubiquity of business cases to transformation efforts, the literature out there isn't actually that great. If you're keen to find out the benefits and costs of digital transformation projects, these are often hidden from public view (often because they go wrong). Many consultancies will write up 'case studies' talking about benefits they helped deliver, but you should always take these with a proverbial pinch of salt; it's in their interests to talk up the work they did. If you can, try and identify a few similar projects to those that you're undertaking, get the details of the project leads, and email and reach out to them for some confidential advice. Suppliers will usually provide you with cost details for new technologies, but be sure to interrogate the full-lifespan costs and all running costs. If you're after a bit more on the technical details of optimism bias, the UK National Audit Office (2013) wrote a valuable report on 'Over-optimism in Government Projects' that's freely available online. And for a more light-hearted, if overly negative, assessment of big projects that failed to deliver benefits, check out Anthony King and Ivor Crewe's *The Blunders of Our Governments* (OneWorld, 2013).

Note

1   Spending Review 2020 (2020) Gov.uk, 15 December, www.gov.uk/government/publications/spending-review-2020-documents/spending-review-2020#shared-outcomes-fund (archived at https://perma.cc/6ZXC-NL8K)

PART THREE

Doing digital

There is no alternative to digital transformation. Visionary companies will carve out new strategic options for themselves – those that don't adapt will fail.

JEFF BEZOS, FORMER AMAZON CEO

Parts 1 and 2 focused on some of the essential foundations of successful digital transformation – setting a strategy and creating a culture that facilitates delivery of the strategy, respectively. In Part 3, we move on to some specific digital considerations. In short, things are going to get a bit more technical – but importantly, hopefully not too much. As a general rule, when it comes to digital transformation, if something sounds too complicated, it's because it's been made too complicated by humans. And as Jeff Bezos' quote demonstrates – we simply cannot avoid digital transformation now. Nevertheless, we should always seek to explain what we're doing in digital transformation simply, because ultimately, humans will be accountable and responsible if things go wrong.

In Chapter 7 we cover the cornerstone that underpins all good digitization efforts: placing real people – users – at the heart of everything. We'll look at approaches to really understand user needs, and techniques to help analyse and articulate them. Chapter 8 covers some core principles that you should use to assess against to ensure you are doing the bare minimum in terms of digital transformation. They should work on both a delivery level (are you doing these things?) and on a governance level (is the organization abiding by these principles?). In Chapters 9 and 10 we address one of the critical questions in technology and the implications of the answer: to build or to buy, respectively. In Chapter 11 we explore the importance of the cloud, APIs and open-source approaches for your digital transformation. Chapter 12 focuses on the broad issue of data science and seeks to get beyond much of the hype surrounding artificial intelligence and instead address the practical benefits of using data to improve decision-making. Chapter 13 addresses the much-vaunted field of innovation, and seeks to provide practical guidance on how to give the best chance of letting innovation flourish in your organization.

07

Understanding your users

Keep it simple. Who are your customers? What do they really need from you? Once you know these answers, deliver on these user needs, brilliantly.

The principle in a nutshell

User-centred design (also known as human-centred design) means putting the needs, wants and desires of humans – be they your customers, your stakeholders or your staff – at the forefront of how you do things. This is achieved by identifying your key users, talking to them to understand their needs, and then designing processes to help meet their needs. This involves constantly and iteratively checking in with your users to ensure their needs are being met, and making improvements as necessary.

User-centred design can be revolutionary. It creates a fundamental mindset shift where value to the business is seen entirely through the lens of users. By truly understanding user needs, you can gain a competitive edge through finding ways to satisfy and delight users. It means that any activity or process that does not fundamentally help to meet a user's needs should be seriously considered for deletion. It is a particularly powerful philosophy when set in a technological context. You will no doubt have experienced technology that is not user-centred. You can recognize it because it is hard to operate. It probably requires an explanation, or worse still, a training course and user manual. This is exactly what, by adopting a user-centred approach, we are aiming to avoid.

What's the problem being addressed?

It was a particular feature of the late 2010s and early 2020s that boardrooms across the globe professed their burning need for 'artificial intelligence' and 'machine learning' to transform their businesses for the better. And yet, a widescale review by the Boston Consulting Group and the MIT Sloan Management Review in 2020 found that only one in ten companies reported seeing significant financial benefits from adopting AI.[1]

No one should be surprised. New technologies frequently disappoint. But the core underlying reason is almost always because executives make the fatal error of believing the technology *in and of itself* would transform things for the better. This is completely the wrong way around. Technology is only a tool. It is the mindset of user-centricity – putting the needs of actual humans first – that enables true transformation. By being user-centred you will *avoid doing technology for technology's sake* and, most importantly, you will make *value to your customers the key element to cherish in your business*. This is a deceptively powerful approach, but the benefits it unlocks can be enormous.

A quick word of warning before we race ahead into how you can become more user-centred. A common critique of user-centred approaches is illustrated by the famous quote widely attributed to the motor car pioneer, Henry Ford: 'If I had asked people what they wanted, they would have said faster horses.' This quote highlights the subtle but important point of difference between *user needs rather than 'user wants'*. In Ford's example, the public may have 'wanted' a better version of what they were used to – horse-drawn carriages – but their actual *underlying need* was to get from one place to another, safely and quickly. *We are interested in the need much more than the want.*

Getting to the heart of your users' needs will allow you to deploy technology effectively and with minimum cost. Your users don't need robots just because your company can afford them.

Putting the principle into action

Who are your users?

Your primary category of users are usually the current or potential 'customers' of your organization. In charitable or public sector organizations, these may often be referred to instead as 'end-users'. Broadly, they are the individuals who buy, use or access products or services from your enterprise.

Depending on the nature of your organization, this description of users may not yet be analytically helpful. A worldwide conglomerate will have lots of different user groups who access its diverse portfolio of products and services. Instead, it is best to think about your user groups at the level of specific digital initiatives or projects. If your store sells to both businesses and consumers, you have two very different user categories (often known as 'business to business' (B2B) and 'business to consumer' (B2C)). And importantly, within these categories, user types will vary. You need to try and understand different characteristics between your users. Often breaking down users along different dimensions (and sometimes using multiple dimensions) can be powerful, for instance:

- *Age:* do your users vary in their needs and preferences by age?
- *Geography:* does your users' location impact their needs?
- *Devices:* do your users tend to use desktops or mobile devices; which web browsers do they use?
- *Comfort with using digital:* does the digital know-how of your users vary, and does this matter?
- *Income or socio-demographic factors:* do wider social or economic issues usefully differentiate between different user groups?

Judgement is required here, and such categorizations should be tested with actual user research, but using such dimensions can help you develop *user personas*, which help to cover a large number of different users. A user persona can take the form of a fictitious person that represents a category of users. It should be based on a composite of characteristics from your user research, and is a powerful way of communicating 'what our users feel and need' to others.

It's important to note that users don't just need to be 'end-users'. 'Internal users', which might be staff, regulators or suppliers, matter too. Ensuring that the products and services that make up your organization are optimized to meet the needs of internal users will lead to better working practices overall.

Doing user research

Once you have a good awareness of the relevant user groups for the improvement you are trying to make, you need to move on to actual user research. The first step you need to take is to recruit users who are willing to take part in the research. To do this, agree your target user groups with your team and then go about finding users. You can use a variety of methods to do this. You may have a customer mailing list that you can use to invite people to take part in research. Or you may need to reach out to colleagues who have closer links with users. Some companies already have established 'customer reference' groups that they can go to directly. It's also completely OK to pay people for their time – either in cash or vouchers.

However, as with all forms of research, you need to be constantly on guard for biases in your research. How can you ensure that the individuals you talk to are representative of your wider user base? Will payment for research skew answers? Do established customer reference groups risk perpetuating the same views? Each circumstance will be different, but it's likely that the risks are real for every approach you take. Where you can mitigate such risks – for instance, by trying to quantify your overall different user groups, and then ensuring you speak to a quantifiably representative sample of users – do so. But where you can't, you will need to be mindful throughout your work and the analysis and conclusions that arise from your user research that some potential risks remain with your underlying data. It's important to be cognisant of these risks, but also not to let them inhibit your work – no data is perfect.

Once you have selected individuals for user research, it's important to be rigorous and consistent in how you undertake your research. You should document and ask users to consent to research. You should also inform users how you intend to use the data that you get from the research. You can utilize user research at many different stages of digital transformation:

- *exploratory:* where you are seeking to understand the underlying needs of a user in relation to a current or potential product, service or transaction (eg, investing money);

- *process-mapping:* where you are aiming to articulate the end-to-end process – also known as a 'user journey' – that an individual goes through as they are seeking to achieve a specific outcome;

- *improvement:* where you are hoping to test a prototype or live service with a user and seeking to understand how they interact with the technology. This should help you spot opportunities for refinement and improvement.

Different techniques can all be deployed in these stages, including:

- *in-depth interviews:* the simplest and most straightforward approach, which involves a user researcher spending time interviewing and discussing with the user, seeking to elicit information through a series of open and closed questions;

- *observations or usability tests:* whereby a user is set a specific task, such as 'move this money from one account to another', and observed by a user researcher, who records the process and any insights arising from the observation;

- *group exercises:* which can take a variety of formats, but multiple users can together be facilitated to help either map out an end-to-end process, or 'card sort' whereby users sort cards with topic names into different groups. This latter technique is particularly useful where organizations are seeking to understand how to display online content meaningfully to customers – the 'card sort' approach helps to understand how a user would taxonomize information, as opposed to how the business would.

Articulating user needs

Your user needs analysis should serve two purposes. First and foremost, it needs to guide your digital transformation and help you decide what sort of digital products and services to develop. But second, it also provides a powerful way to communicate to the rest of your business and stakeholders what your users really think and feel. As such, from the deep complexity of human needs and emotions, we need a simple way to describe user needs. Thankfully, two techniques are at hand.

A simple yet powerful approach is to describe your user needs as follows:

As a... [which type of user?]

I need... [what does the user want to do?]

So that... [why does the user want to do this?]

So, if you were investigating the scope for a new procurement platform for universities, you may describe high-level user needs as such:

As a... finance director at a university

I need... a reliable and efficient means of buying goods and services with confidence

So that... I can purchase quickly and effectively the goods and services needed to provide university services, and gain the necessary documentation required for the purchase.

Another, more detailed way of capturing and articulating user needs can be through developing *empathy maps*. These are best completed by spending time with a user as they either take you through or talk you through the journey they go on to achieve a specific outcome. You should then capture relevant observations across the dimensions shown in Figure 7.1.

By capturing insight across these categories, you should be building an evidence base for where digital transformation can make things better for users. For instance, a user with low digital confidence making an online planning application to their local council might have an empathy map like the one in Figure 7.2.

In the example in Figure 7.2, by identifying the salient issues for the user, any future changes should be made that prioritize the user experience and remove the pains, fears and struggles outlined.

Visualizing user journeys

It's also important to visualize how your users interact with your organization. You should do this initially to understand the current state and therefore where and how things can be improved. And you should also visualize user journeys to help set out the future state. This can help to communicate to people how they may need to work differently going forward.

FIGURE 7.1 An empathy map

THINKS What is occupying the user's thoughts through this process?	FEELS What is the user's emotional state during the process?	PAINS What are the fears, frustrations and obstacles facing the user?
SAYS What does the user say out loud during the interview or observation?	DOES What are the actions the user takes during the process?	GAINS What does success look like for the user?

FIGURE 7.2 An example empathy map for a 'low digital confidence' user

THINKS Can't someone else do this for me? Isn't that what I pay my taxes for?	FEELS Confused by the process. Worried about doing the wrong thing.	PAINS Fear of making a mistake. Distrust of giving personal details online.
SAYS I feel disenfranchised by the need to do this online. Why can't I do this in person?	DOES Calls up the council. Directed to a website. Struggles to complete the form unaided.	GAINS Successfully lodging an application in a timely manner.

One approach is to create *rich picture* journey map visualizations. These provide a high-level, end-to-end overview of a process. They should capture the key users, the steps they go through, how they interact with the process, and any key points of data capture or data flows. A rich picture should be simple yet visually compelling. An example, based around our previous procurement platform scenario, is shown in Figure 7.3.

Rich pictures are useful in creating a simple, clear approach for how a service currently does (or does not) work, and how it can be better in the future. Sometimes more information and granularity is required, though, and for this, *service blueprints* can be hugely valuable. A service blueprint outlines, by different elements in an end-to-end process, the steps taken and the users involved. A legend can be used to record different categories of steps within a process. If you're able to quantify volumes going through each part of the process (if you're seeking to develop a customer service chatbot, it would be important to quantify the volumes of customer contacts for each different service or query, for instance), this will make your understanding of the service even better. Again, service blueprints are vital in discerning improvements that can be made to the current state, and in clearly explaining new roles in a future state.

Figure 7.4 gives an example service blueprint using specialized software, although good old-fashioned Post-It notes can more than suffice.

FIGURE 7.3 Example of a rich picture journey map of a procurement platform

Rich pictures displaying user journeys

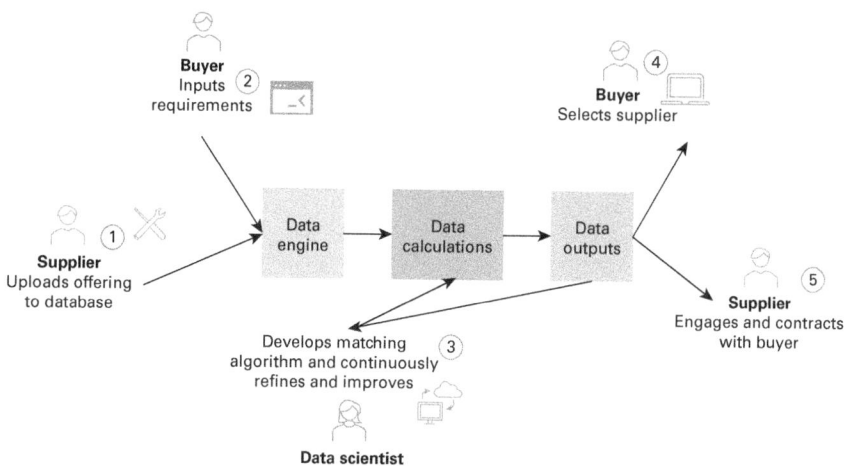

FIGURE 7.4 Example of a procurement platform service blueprint

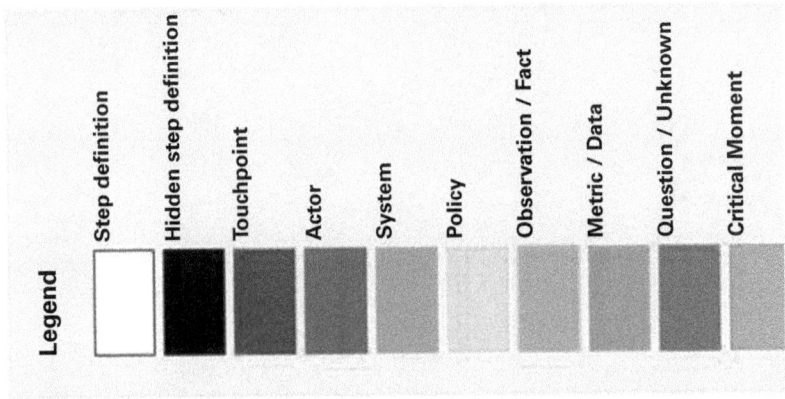

Procurement platform blueprint

End-to-end ideal future state process

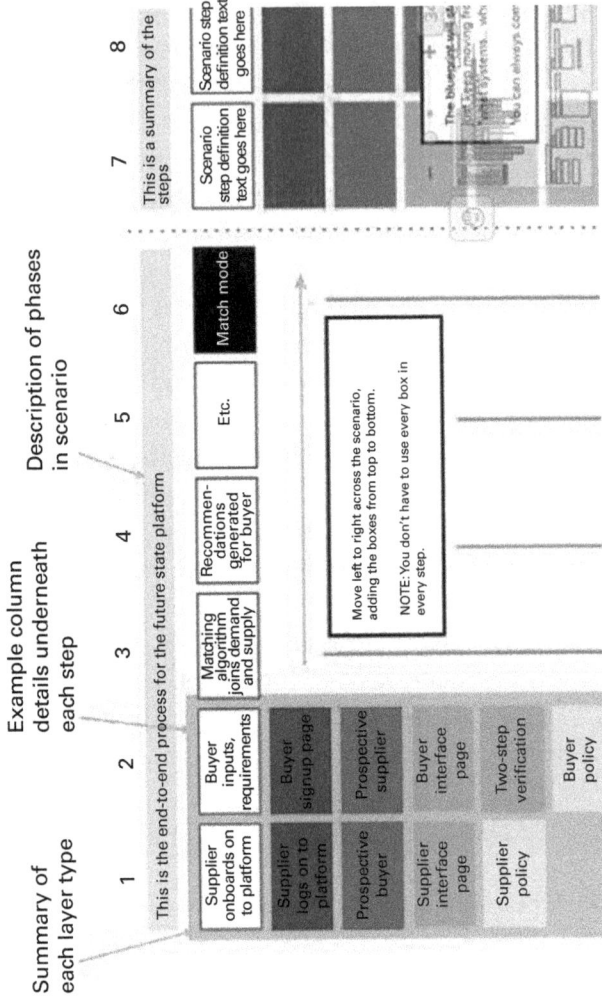

Summary of each layer type

Example column details underneath each step

Description of phases in scenario

	1	2	3	4	5	6	7	8
							This is a summary of the steps	
							Scenario step definition text goes here	Scenario step definition text goes here

This is the end-to-end process for the future state platform

Supplier onboards on to platform	Buyer inputs, requirements	Matching algorithm joins demand and supply	Recommen-dations generated for buyer	Etc.	Match mode
Supplier logs on to platform	Buyer signup page				
Prospective buyer	Prospective supplier				
Supplier interface page	Buyer interface page				
Supplier policy	Two-step verification				
	Buyer policy				

Move left to right across the scenario, adding the boxes from top to bottom.

NOTE: You don't have to use every box in every step.

Legend

☐	Step definition
■	Hidden step definition
■	Touchpoint
■	Actor
■	System
■	Policy
■	Observation / Fact
■	Metric / Data
■	Question / Unknown
■	Critical Moment

USER RESEARCH DURING PANDEMICS

The Covid-19 pandemic that began in 2020 initially posed significant challenges to user researchers across the world. Many worried that the human interaction and subtle physical cues that are picked up from face-to-face user research would be missed and make remote user research less powerful. Undoubtedly challenges were posed, most notably in ensuring representation for digitally uncomfortable users (in these instances, socially distanced user research was nonetheless found to work). However, video-conferencing technology did allow user research to continue, and potentially even more quickly, easily and accessible than before. The fact that user research no longer required users or researchers to travel opened new avenues for connections. In short, user research and its approaches proved remarkably resilient to the challenges raised by Covid-19.

Where next?

Remember user research is valuable at multiple points in your digital transformation. You should use it to work out what's wrong and needs improving. But it's also vital in continuously iterating and improving your digital technologies, and in communicating to stakeholders the changes you are undertaking.

Make sure to build in time for user research throughout your digital transformation work. User research is typically the domain of skilled and trained individuals known as 'user researchers' (see Chapter 16 for more on such specialist roles), but it's critically important that all members of your team engage in and undertake user research. There's no substitute for getting to know your users – it will keep you honest and focused on where the true value lies in digital transformation.

Once you have a good sense of user needs, make sure to translate these into practical action in your digital strategy – most obviously through guiding your decision-making. You don't want to get into a vicious cycle where you feel the need to continuously conduct user research without ever advancing things, 'in case our users' needs change'. User research is brilliant, but you can have too much of a good thing.

BRINGING THE PRINCIPLE TO LIFE
The limits of data-led user personas at Amazon

How can a heavy focus on data-led decision-making marry up with the softer, more human emphasis that user research brings? What are the trade-offs? Where do judgement calls need to be made?

Amazon is undoubtedly one of the most data-rich companies to have ever existed. It is also an organization that places a high premium on user-centricity. However, in a fascinating book by former employee Tamara Adlin, the importance of user personas needing to be 'accurate but not precise' become startlingly apparent.[2]

As Adlin recalls, 'We could try to sort and re-analyze and statistically re-assess and model and segment [huge datasets to generate personas] to our heart's content, but we couldn't really find anything useful.' The reason was there was simply *too much data* and the team generating personas was trying to cover too much. The breadth of Amazon's service range (even in the early 2000s) was neither useful nor helpful to apply a data-rich lens to developing user personas. As Adlin writes:

> Useful personas have to be *precise* (in other words, a persona has to be male OR female, a professional horse jockey OR the manager of a network operations center). This is why 'middle-aged, ex-urban women with children' can't be a persona, but Elizabeth, who lives in Orange, New Jersey, and has two kids named Ethan and Emily, can. And because they have to be precise, they can't really be *accurate*: you can't accurately describe a set of data using a single person. This is probably the biggest reason we couldn't create data-driven personas for all of Amazon.

This is a salutary tale that highlights the complexity of user research. User research has its origins in the social sciences and, specifically, ethnographic research. Its methodologies are deliberately qualitative and considered. Particularly in data-rich environments such as technology, there is a belief that the data and 'numbers' can tell us everything we need to know about customers and stakeholders, but user-centricity in general and Adlin's Amazon tale in particular highlights the importance of retaining a focus on real, lived human experiences. Particular power comes in combining the qualitative techniques of user research with sensible, sensitive quantification – quantifying the time taken in delays in a user journey, or the cost of errors, or in ensuring a sufficiently representative group of users being interviewed.

Tips and tricks

- Close your eyes and just visualize the critical customers, stakeholders and internal staff in your organization. Who comes first to mind? These are probably your main user groups.

- Within your largest and most important user groups, consider which dimensions are important and may be useful in segmenting users by different needs and preferences.

- Who is undertaking the user research? Make sure they are experienced, knowledgeable and follow consistent methodological approaches. User research may seem simple, but this is deceptive: there is art in truly getting to understand what the underlying needs of your users are.

- Don't get confused with *wants* and *needs*. There can be value in serving customer *wants* very well, but this is unlikely to lead to real transformation. Getting to the true *need* is the key to unlocking benefits.

- Visualize what your users want and showcase this in your organization. This will help people understand how you're thinking about digital transformation from a human-centred perspective.

What you might say in your next meeting

Who are our users and what do they need?

We can't serve the world. We need to consider who our most important users are and how we can best serve them.

People aren't data. They are humans with feelings and emotions and needs. By truly appreciating this, we will deliver a better service to them.

Technology is there to serve humans, not the other way around.

Technology can help us do user research well, especially if we're restricted in human contact.

Where you can find out more

One book above all has revolutionized how many technologists think about user-centred design. Don Norman's *The Design of Everyday Things* (MIT

Press, 2013), first published in 1988 but continuously updated subsequently, is the ultimate explainer for how user-centred design, ethnographic approaches and making brilliant products and services that are in tune with human needs can transform the world for the better.

Notes

1 Ransbotham, S, *et al* (2020) *Expanding AI's Impact with Organizational Learning*, Boston Consulting Group, 20 October, www.bcg.com/publications/2020/is-your-company-embracing-full-potential-of-artificial-intelligence (archived at https://perma.cc/T84M-5K3J)
2 Pruitt, J and Adlin, T (2006) *The Persona Lifecycle: Keeping people in mind throughout product design*, Morgan Kaufmann, Burlington, MA

08

Doing the bare minimum

Getting the basics right is never enough. But it's literally the least you can – and need to – do.

The principle in a nutshell

The digital landscape is constantly evolving. Huge transformations have occurred since the post-war period alone. The 1960s were dominated by large mainframe computers. The 1980s saw a revolution through the creation of personal devices. The 1990s brought the seismic power of the internet. The 2000s witnessed the advent of cloud computing. The 2010s heralded the rise of platform models, enabled by connections through application program interfaces (APIs). And the 2020s have seen virtual models and remote working become the norm. These enormous changes highlight the impossibility of 'fixing the basics' because the basics are always changing. However, there are what you might call 'no regrets' moves that every organization should ensure it has in place to do the bare minimum. These are not set in stone, so consider them principles rather than a binary done/not done checklist. As always, every work environment is slightly different, so judgement is always required.

What's the problem being addressed?

There's a lot to cover in the 'no regrets' categories, so we'll keep this brief. In essence, what follows are a set of defence mechanisms to avoid something going badly wrong. Of course, these are all designed to ensure the *foundations are in place for your successful digital transformation.* But there's also an element of protecting you and your reputation. Anecdotally, IT is up there with HR for the department that most consistently loses out in the corporate 'blame game'. These steps should at the very least give you some good protection.

Putting the principles into action

Design around specific use cases

In Chapter 7 we covered the monumental importance of starting all your technology considerations with your users in mind. And so the next step is to ensure that everything your organization does can be related back to a specific user need, also known as a 'use case'. If you can't articulate what use case your technology serves, it's likely time to decommission it or reconfigure how it works.

Have a clear handle on the technology stack

A technology stack – also known as a 'solutions stack' – refers to all of the systems required to run a service, or the services within an organization. If you've ever looked at a diagram drawn by someone from IT with lots of boxes, cylinders and lines, this is probably a technology stack. It may look daunting, but don't let it overwhelm you. The Appendix covers a simplified version of a stack, and in truth there are lots of different ways and schools of thought regarding how to define stacks. Nonetheless, a stack usually consists of elements covering:

DATA AND OPERATING ENVIRONMENT

Operating systems: these should be determined based on the type of technology being run, and your organization's expertise and comfort with the different types of operating system. Common examples include iOS, Android, Python, Ruby. Depending on the complexity of your organization, you may run multiple operating systems.

Servers: these are where your applications are based. Servers can be physical or virtual, distributed or centralized. They will allow you to send, receive and access data. Depending on how they are constructed, servers give you the capacity to scale your services according to need. This scaling ability, and the reduced cost of server storage, has led most progressive organizations to choose cloud hosting services. Main server providers include Amazon Web Services, Microsoft Azure and Google Cloud. You may still find that for some older technologies in your organization you host services on your own, physical, internal servers.

Data storage and retrieval: this allows you to store and retrieve the data processed by your services. Data pipelines, data warehouses and relational and non-relational databases all fall under this category. Your user needs should guide your choices here. Relational databases (where the data is structured) are great if you know fairly precisely what data you want to access and in what format. Conversely, while non-relational databases offer more flexibility, more work is required to retrieve data in an easily interrogatable form. MySQL, PostgreSQL and MongoDB are all examples that fall in this stack layer.

Frameworks: these are a collection of languages or code libraries that help to guide how your technology is developed. It's not essential to pre-agree a framework, but it can help keep control of your stack. Ruby on Rails, .NET or Django are popular frameworks to use in data and operating environments.

FRONT-END USER EXPERIENCE

Frameworks: similar to data and operating environment or 'back-end' frameworks, these provide a set of guidelines for how your users will experience and interact with the technology. AngularJS or Bootstrap provide toolkits for front-end frameworks. The overall desired user experience will most likely vary depending on your choice of framework. Frameworks differ in terms of the size of their developer communities, tutorial guides, overall design approach, how customizable templates are, availability of linked modules, security considerations, support levels and overall functionality. Generally speaking, the end-user experience most obviously differs when relating to experience when using mobile devices; some frameworks more naturally deliver what is known as a 'responsive mobile-first experience' than others.

CONNECTIONS AND INTEROPERABILITY

'Interoperability' – a much vaunted term – generally just means connecting computers and systems together. This can be achieved through a variety of ways and at different levels within a technology stack.

Middleware: sometimes referred to as 'plumbing', these connect operating systems and applications together. They are usually hidden from the end-user but are vital in moving data across your stack. Varying forms of middleware are available, covering everything from database connections to security authentication.

Abstraction layers: also help to join parts of your technology stack together. The layers separate out steps in a given process, and multiple layers may be required. URLs and domain names are a common form of abstraction layer; the process here is to convert alphabetic website names to numeric IP addresses.

Application program interfaces: a popular form of abstraction layer, these are tools that help connect applications together, which can help join together the user experience. Google APIgee allows management and development of APIs.

Web applications: one of the most amazing developments of the internet has been the manner in which it has afforded simple, cheap and effective connections between web browsers (such as Chrome or Firefox), web servers and database servers. These ensure application functionality without having to download or install programs.

BUSINESS REQUIREMENTS

Performance monitoring: these help to monitor overall performance of your stack. AppDynamics or Datadog are popular examples here.

Business intelligence: these tools focus at a higher level of overview, usually looking to understand overall company or business unit performance. PowerBI, Tableau or Qlik are commonly used.

Behavioural analytics: much more focused on user behaviours than overall business analytics. Google Analytics is a prime example here, which helps to track and analyse user actions at various stages in your processes. Things that you would wish behavioural analytics to inform you of are whether customers leave a website quickly (known as the 'bounce rate'), engage with pages ('click-through rate'), undertake a desired outcome ('conversation rate') or unsubscribe ('churn rate').

Productivity and operations: these are tools which help your employees work more effectively. Examples include Atlassian Confluence, which is focused on agile ways of working, and the Google GSuite or Microsoft 365, which provide many apps to help organizations be more effective.

Commercial and marketing: focused on improving sales or income, customer relationship management tools such as Salesforce are frequently used.

The above list is not exhaustive. Your technology stack might include apps and software that help with workflow, human resources issues, agile DevOps (a project management approach for developer teams running live services) or more. The key point is your tech stack will define your operations and organizational culture. It's very hard to have consistent ways of working if different teams in your organization are all using different tools. And it's even harder to have control, oversight and assurance that data is being properly and securely stored when tech stacks become unwieldy (as a rule of thumb, if it requires a special project every time you wish to identify all the components in your tech stack, it's probably unwieldy). Keep a close eye on the tech stack, and look to rationalize and decommission parts of it when you can.

Embrace the cloud – tightly

Most organizations are now moving their data and operations to the cloud, rather than on in-house servers. The benefits of in-house servers include keeping your critical data close to you, giving you physical and tangible backups of your key data, and better control during disasters – such as if internet connectivity goes down. The benefits of cloud servers are reduced capital and hardware costs, improved ease of scaling up, and remote access of data from any device. In addition, most backup and disaster recovery risks can be well mitigated in the cloud. A hybrid model, for some organizations, may be entirely appropriate; keeping some data and services backed up with physical servers (if internet connectivity going down is a real and frequent issue, for instance).

Notwithstanding, it will be hard to find any company that's serious about digital transformation that doesn't have the cloud as a major part of its strategy. The important point here is to keep a handle on what goes in the cloud. It's increasingly easy for teams to set up their own software-as-a-service accounts (see Chapter 11 for more on this) for new technologies, and store potentially sensitive data in these cloud-based accounts without anyone knowing. In addition, while most cloud storage costs start out very cheap, inevitably with volume, usage and time the costs go up – so keep a watchful eye on this.

Establish clear data flows

The focus on user needs can risk putting lots of focus on the 'front end' of digital, without paying due attention to the 'back end'. As you develop your service blueprints and user journeys (Chapter 7), it's important to map out how the data needs to flow throughout the processes. Data movement will take various form:

- *inputting:* such as a customer entering personal information;
- *ingestion:* where data may be moved from one source to another, often for analytical or storage purposes;
- *transformation:* post-ingestion, data may need to be processed or 'transformed' in order to cleanse to be ready for use;
- *calculation or analysis:* where data is analysed, often bringing together multiple sources of data; data may need to be *retrieved* from a data source in order for the analysis to be conducted;
- *data visualization or presentation:* where data is presented back to a user, to help answer a question, such as understanding customer behaviour.

By mapping and keeping an eye on data flows, it should help to guard against data getting lost or accessed by the wrong users.

Ensure the user experience is joined up

As we covered in Chapter 7, most user needs are complex and rarely served by a single process. As such, there are usually connections to multiple services. To give as great an experience as possible, minimize 'dead ends' that users experience. For instance, in many countries, moving house requires various forms to be filled in. Much of this can be done online. However, some documents need to be printed, signed with a wet signature, and then posted somewhere. A code may then be sent back (by post) and the digital process restarted. This is a poor user experience. Aiming to make experiences end-to-end is the goal.

Make things accessible

You should design your digital services to minimize excluding people. For public services, these need to be universal, so they should be designed so *everyone* can access them. This may necessitate telephone helplines or face-to-face services to aid completion of the digital services. In the private sector, this isn't always the case. A digital-only wills and probate service will only need to design services for customers who are digitally savvy; by design they are excluding customers with low digital confidence. That's probably OK in this instance. But remember that a digitally comfortable customer may have accessibility requirements too. Colour blindness, dyslexia, low literacy levels, requirements for language translation or visual impairment are just some of the key accessibility considerations you need to make.

Keep an eye on your hardware

Technology relies on hardware and devices. These require careful procurement (see Chapter 10), but also ongoing servicing and decommissioning. Particularly when it comes to decommissioning, you need to ensure devices don't go missing or fall into the wrong hands. Unencrypted or poorly secured devices can pose a real risk. Keep a register of who has what hardware, its state and condition, and when it's ready to be retired, make sure it is.

Focus on privacy and security

Data breaches or cybersecurity attacks should be near the top of any digitally progressive organization's risk register. From the outset, you need to design in consent mechanisms to ensure any user data you hold is done so legitimately and legally. Regulations, such as the EU General Data Protection Regulation, provide clear guidance, although these will vary from territory to territory and you need to stay abreast of changes. Cybersecurity also needs to be at the front of mind; this requires guidance, training and ongoing reviews and testing to ensure you are prepared for eventualities. We will cover this in more detail in Chapter 14.

Plan for disasters

What happens if one of your servers goes down? Or if you suffer a major cyber attack? How will your organization continue to function under such scenarios? Planning for disasters and developing business continuity plans is a must-have. You may be lucky and not have to deal with these, but you need to make sure you're ready and prepared in case you do.

Put analytics front of mind

Since the mid-2010s the rise of considerations around 'big data' has made us all much more conscious about the potential of data science and analytics. While some of the early promise has yet to bear fruit, you should always think how data analysis can help improve your digital operations. What do you want to know now and what do you want to know in the future? Once you have a grasp on this, work backwards to ensure your data flows are structured in a way to help to answer such questions.

Set standards and policies – and enforce them

Technology can be overwhelming, yet every single person in your organization will have some relationship with it. You need to provide them with standards and guidance about how to use technology appropriately – which software or products to use, how and when to use devices and for what purpose, how to ensure their operations are safe and secure. Your enterprise should develop clear standards that are easily accessible, understandable, updated and distributed to all. And if someone breaches these standards, there need to be consequences to demonstrate the importance of following them.

Use spend controls as a gateway

While it's probably true that on the whole, most organizations should spend more rather than less on digital, they should nonetheless spend it wisely. If you are part of a central digital function, it may be prudent and appropriate to create a 'spend controls' function whereby new technology spend is only approved centrally. This will help to both reinforce standards and policies (only technologies which are compliant are approved) and save potentially huge amounts. The UK government saved £353 million in 2018/19 alone through its central government spend controls function.[1]

Maximize functionality

When you do buy something, make sure you use it to its full potential. Organizations frequently buy duplicative goods and services without fully maximizing the functions and services they are already paying for (how many different analytics platforms or virtual conferencing products does your organization pay for, for instance?). Again, this may not just save money; it could make for a clearer, simpler technology stack that is easier to manage.

Put a premium on governance and accountability

Getting governance right is imperative. Every organization should – at least – have a senior board member who is responsible for data protection. In addition, your digital transformation needs to be clear in accountabilities, articulating who is on the hook for which elements of the transformation. Scrutiny needs to be applied to digital standards, policies and technologies with a governance structure set up that supports this. Starting with ensuring that the principles covered in this chapter are addressed would not be a bad first line of enquiry for these governance structures.

Make sure you have digital leadership and capability at the top (at least)

Ideally, you will have sufficient digital capability in your company so that you are not entirely reliant on external service providers and contractors. But at the very least, you need to have experienced, knowledgeable digital leadership at the top of the organization. Digital, data and technology responsibility should lie at the executive level of the organization. Pushing them a level down (such as reporting to a chief operating officer or chief finance officer) risks minimizing their importance and may cause critical issues to get missed. Digital merits a seat at the top table.

Where next?

These principles are not a simple checklist. But you can consider them general considerations that you should check in on, before, during and after your digital transformation. There may well be good reasons for deviating from recommended practice within the principles – for instance, you may choose not to maximize the functionality of a given piece of software because your organization is intending on decommissioning it in the near future. And when these reasons and instances arise, you should make sure to clearly document and articulate why you are making these choices to stakeholders.

Some of the principles covered required a good understanding of the existing culture and practices of your organization. Your technology stack, for instance, is highly likely to be formed from existing elements of the stack. There may be some instances where you have a 'greenfield' opportunity to develop a new stack entirely from scratch, but in most companies, this is a luxury few can afford. As such, make sure you have a good understanding of where you are against each of the principles now, before committing to major changes in the future.

These principles cover the sorts of questions that a knowing non-executive director or interested outside party – such as an acquirer or an investor – might ask, and so you should be ready with a good answer.

BRINGING THE PRINCIPLE TO LIFE
Introducing technology standards and spend controls

A common feature of leading digital governments in the early 2020s was spend controls and common standards. According to the OECD Digital Government Index, nations including Denmark, Norway, Portugal and the United Kingdom all had cross-government spend controls for new technologies in place.[2]

The United Kingdom was the pioneer of this model. From 2010, it introduced spend controls whereby key central government departments – approximately 20 in total – had to formally report their intended technology developments and expenditure. These would then be assessed and assured by internal experts from the Government Digital Service, a department within the UK Cabinet Office.

The first part of the spend controls process involved creating a 15–18-month pipeline of proposed digital developments. This pipeline would then be triaged. Any expenditure over a certain threshold – usually £100,000 for digital spend (ie new services) or £5 million in technology spend (ie hardware and infrastructure) would be in scope for spend controls. In addition, items that were deemed 'contentious in nature' would also need to be considered. These included:

- contracts over £100 million in value;
- automatic contract extensions;
- new hosting contracts greater than two years;
- investments in 'emerging technologies like artificial intelligence, machine learning, blockchain and quantum computing'.

These pipeline activities would need to be assessed by an internal department assurance board, which would then need to make a formal recommendation as to whether to proceed with the proposed work. The recommendation would then ultimately be reviewed by the internal spend control central team which sat in the Cabinet Office.

Critics of this approach argue it creates bureaucracy and can slow down decision-making (indeed, during the Covid-19 pandemic, many spend control requirements were temporarily lifted to allow fast action). However, the process also affords the ability to ensure common standards are followed – in the UK, this is part of the assurance process – and allows good engagement between departments, and consistent medium- and long-term planning. Between 2013 and 2018, over £1 billion was estimated to have been saved through this approach by the UK government alone.[3]

Tips and tricks

- Use these principles as a guide throughout your digital transformation. If you're not abiding by them, make sure you know why.

- Make sure your senior stakeholders are well sighted on these principles and agree with them.

- Some organizations like to publish their working principles openly. This can help attract new recruits, investors and provide some positive marketing.

- Talk to other companies to hear how they address each of these principles. See what you can learn from others – both their successes and mistakes.

- Stay honest. It's better to fail to meet a principle but be honest about it rather than pretend you are meeting it.

What you might say in your next meeting

Doing the bare minimum will never be enough. But it's a decent start.

The landscape changes too quickly to set hard and fast rules, but these principles can guide us on our digital transformation journey.

Do we have a firm handle on our technology stack?

Who approves what gets bought and implemented here?

Does our board have a good grasp on whether we're following good principles?

Where you can find out more

The UK Government Digital Service publishes its Service Standard with which new digital services need to conform.[4] These are slightly different from the principles outlined in this chapter as they mainly concern themselves with user-facing transactional services, but are nonetheless a good resource when considering setting standards. If you are keen to learn more about technology stacks, websites such as Crunchbase, StackShare or Heap can give you an excellent insight into what popular companies use.

Notes

1 UK Government Digital Service (2019) Spend-controls: saving money and making things better, 16 July, gds.blog.gov.uk/2019/07/16/spend-controls-saving-money-and-making-things-better/ (archived at https://perma.cc/QZ28-LHA3)

2 The OECD Digital Government Framework (2019) www.oecd-ilibrary.org/docserver/f64fed2a-en.pdf?expires=1618842529&id=id&accname=guest&checksum=40E34BBF9E78A8679ADD623C70EB1E8E (archived at https://perma.cc/4CK2-N9GY)

3 UK Government Digital Service (2018) We're improving the digital and IT spend controls process, 2 May, gds.blog.gov.uk/2018/05/02/were-improving-the-digital-and-it-spend-controls-process/ (archived at https://perma.cc/QY6U-9JMD)

4 UK Government Digital Service Service Standard, www.gov.uk/service-manual/service-standard (archived at https://perma.cc/UGV5-XRKV)

09

Building new services

Doing digital in-house can give you control and freedom, and potentially reduce costs.

The principle in a nutshell

Digital transformation is hard, and doing digital transformation in-house may seem hugely daunting. But it can unlock huge benefits when done well, giving you control and autonomy in a way that relying on external suppliers never can.

Building new services can take two forms. It can be done either through dedicated teams of software developers who are in-house, permanent staff in your company. Or through a mixed economy model, where a few key roles – usually a product owner or service owner – are done by someone in your organization, with external contractors hired for specific tasks who report to the internal lead. This latter model is often the most realistic. Software developers are at a premium and you may not be able to attract the right people on a permanent basis, so this mixed economy model gives you overall control, while affording some flexibility in resourcing your efforts.

It won't always be sensible to build new services in-house. Usually it makes most sense if you have some existing digital capability that you can build on, if you're developing services that are either completely new or need to be very bespoke to your organization and users, or if there's a real risk you could get locked in to a relationship with an external supplier for many years if you rely on them for the development.

What's the problem being addressed?

To build or to buy is a big decision. Building is neither for everyone nor the faint-hearted. But it certainly separates truly digitally progressive organizations from others. If you're thinking about doing things in-house, consider:

- *How tech-first are you?* Thinking back to the archetypes in Chapter 2, taking control of your digital destiny makes most sense for those organizations for whom technology is a key part of their value proposition.

- *Is the solution novel?* If no one on the market is able to provide a pre-existing solution, this might be a good opportunity to try and create the new solution yourself. But you should also consider whether the reason nothing exists already is because it's impossible to do or a terrible idea.

- ***Does the service need considerable customization to your users' needs?*** There may be pre-existing generic solutions out there, but if they need to be greatly configured and customized to your situation, it may be more cost-efficient in the long run to develop yourself.

- ***Do you have the infrastructure in place to host the service?*** Running a digital service requires storing and hosting data, processing data and complying with regulations, upgrading and fixing issues, and providing wrap-around support. If you don't have these in place – or intend to have them – the whole idea might be a non-starter.

- *How important is having control to you?* This will vary depending on what element or processes in your organization are being digitized. Taking things in-house is best when you feel having control and flexibility is critical. If you're thinking about whether you can scale up a service to lots of users following rapid iteration, this is extremely hard to do if you're in a multi-year contract with an external provider. By contrast, if you're running the service in-house, you should be in much greater control of your own destiny.

Putting the principle into action

Building great, well-functioning digital products and services requires blending an overarching philosophy of innovation, experimentation and user-centricity with a rigorous and well-defined methodology.

Use service design thinking

Once you've made a decision to develop something in-house, you should embrace service design approaches. A lot of this means being user-centred, which we've covered in depth already, but it's not just that.

Service design means thinking about journeys end-to-end and top-to-bottom. What is the end outcome your users are trying to access? How will they know when they've achieved it? How will you know if the service is working? In addition, you need to consider how the service forms part of your wider digital ecosystem. How do services link together? How does data flow across them? What are the interdependencies between services? It's vital that you can answer all of these questions before you start any digital build work.

The use of the term 'service' is important because it conveys a certain mindset that works on multiple levels. First and foremost, you are providing a valuable and reliable service to your users. Their experience is of prime importance and should supersede other considerations. Second, it helps to emphasize that technology is always part of a wider end-to-end journey. It should not just be a one-off transaction, that is, I have provided data to X. A great service, even as simple a process as inputting data, should inform the users that their data has been successfully inputted, for instance.

While much digital parlance talks about products and platforms, these are also fundamentally service generators. Uber is a platform for matching a user's need to move from A to B with drivers who can facilitate that need; but it's also an end-to-end service that encompasses the entire user journey, and beyond (such as if you're giving feedback). Similarly, digital products also provide services. Video home doorbells of course provide specific product functionality – I can see X on demand – but they are part of a wider service for users: 'I want to know what's going on at my house so I can be confident it's safe and secure.' Having service design thinking in mind will help you make the leap from just building something that 'just about works' to something that can truly delight people and make them come back for more.

Get the right skills and capabilities

People build digital services and you need the right ones in place to do so. Figure 9.1 demonstrates a best-practice approach for developing services. We discussed in Chapter 4 the various key digital roles, but it's an important point to stress that you will almost certainly need – at some point, in some guise – *all of these roles* to be made available to you:

- product/service owner/manager;
- delivery manager;
- business analyst;
- user researcher;
- service designer;
- technical architect;
- software engineer/developer;
- data scientist.

In addition, depending on the nature of your service, you may require content designers, who will focus on ensuring you have great written communications and copy that meets user needs. Depending on the complexity of your data, you may also need data engineers to ensure data is stored, processed and cleansed appropriately (although data scientists and software engineers may be able to do much of this).

You may not need all of these roles at the same time, but you may need more than one of each role at different points. In the early phases of service development – discovery to early alpha phases – you can usually rely on the first half of the family of roles, the more user-facing skills. However, as you quickly get into building services, the more technical roles are utterly essential. It's no use having a beautifully designed front end of a digital service if, technically, it doesn't or cannot work.

FIGURE 9.1   An agile design project management approach

Phase	Discovery	Alpha	Beta	Live	Retirement
Outcomes	Define the problem; understand user needs; identify potential solutions; quantify the 'size of the prize' in solving the problem	Develop and test potential solutions with users	Build out a single, preferred working solution, made available to users	Run and continuously improve a live, freely accessible service	Decommission service; share best practice; secure data

Sourcing these skills is covered in depth in Chapter 16. Strategically, however, you need to consider whether you are going to:

• host a dedicated, full-capability digital team in your organization; or
• recruit key digital specialists in a mixed economy model.

In the first model, this makes sense if you have a pipeline of activity to justify a full-time team, can afford the salaries and present a sufficiently compelling proposition for what is scarce talent. It's completely viable in the age of remote working and cloud servers to have many of your digital team off-shored or near-shored, and this may reduce costs. As always, you do need to do good due diligence and ensure there is a strong cultural alignment and that your on-site and off-site teams can work well together.

In the latter model, this is particularly sensible if you only have a limited pipeline of digital activity. A mixed economy model should allow you to scale up as demand requires. You may pay slightly more for agencies and consultancies than if they were internal permanent staff, but you don't need to hire them for as long. When considering which roles to have in-house, it's best to try and focus on the most senior ones: service or product owners, delivery managers or technical architects being key. These in-house staff can in essence be the commissioners and managers of any external contractors in the mixed economy model.

Use the agile design process

The agile project management approach to building new services has been tried, tested and perfected in companies such as Apple, IBM and Procter & Gamble. While descriptions may vary slightly, the approach should follow five broad phases.

DISCOVERY
Fundamentally, this is where you define the problem you are trying to solve. Discoveries should be short, sharp and end up with a proposed solution or solutions to the identified problem that you are recommending be taken forward for further work. Durations will vary depending on need and circumstances, but a good discovery can be done in as little as 4 weeks and should not really exceed 12 weeks.

In a discovery, you'll be defining the problem space (such as reducing customer churn), identifying your key user groups, and most importantly, going out and speaking to users. Your user research will result in artefacts that help you understand user needs better, and therefore how to address them. These could include journey maps, rich pictures and user stories and persons – all things we covered in Chapter 7.

Once you've thoroughly understood user needs, you should be in a position to brainstorm potential solutions – usually digital ones, but not necessarily always – to meet these needs. You're likely to end up with a long list of possible answers, which needs whittling down.

The discovery phase should also seek to answer quantifiable business questions such as: how much is this problem worth to us?; what will be the benefits of solving this problem?; and what proposed solutions are more likely to meet our overall user needs?

By the end of the discovery phase, you should know:

- whether there is sufficient business merit in continuing to an alpha phase;
- what the specific problem to be solved is, and a small (no more than three, and possibly one) number of potential solutions to the problem;
- whether the likely benefits of solving the problem outweigh the likely potential costs.

ALPHA

The alpha phase is all about testing different solutions. By the end of the phase, you should have a clear preference for a solution that gets taken forward to be built in the beta phase.

A solid alpha timescale can be anywhere between 8 and 16 weeks. During this time you and the team will be doing three things, mainly.

First, building prototypes of digital services. These can be lo-fi (just wireframe diagrams and hand-drawn or digitally mocked up screens) or fully coded and 'clickable' (ie functional to some extent). You should focus as much on the front end as the back end. In other words, make sure that the user journey is seamless, but also that the data flows are fit for purpose, that data can move between different systems as necessary, and that storage, hosting and security requirements are thought of.

Second, you will do a huge amount of user testing of these prototypes. You need to get your worked examples in front of real, live users. You want them to spot errors, bugs, dead ends. This is the phase where you need problems to be identified. If your users aren't finding improvements that you need to act upon, you're probably doing the user testing wrong. Finding users for whom the back-end considerations matter is critical. These may be staff working in other parts of the business who rely on the digital service to provide them with data or insights. Check with them as much as with your external users that the prototyped service actually works.

Third, you should be undertaking business analysis to understand the implications of your changes. How do different solutions affect costs? Will the changes make things more efficient? What will be the best technology stack within which to develop the service? Do the benefits you identified in the discovery phase still stack up? If not, do you need to check in with your corporate seniors to get their support to still continue?

By the end of the alpha, you need a clear, unambiguous proposal and technical blueprint for what you're bringing forward into the next phase: beta.

BETA

During beta is when you actually build the service. It may be helpful to do this in two phases: a 'private beta' phase, where the service is developed for a small (low hundreds, for instance) number of users; and then a 'public beta' phase, where it's opened up to your full array of customers. Betas can vary significantly in length: from 4 months to 12 months is not uncommon.

The beta phase will be much more developer-heavy than previous phases. User testing will continue to be important, and the product or service owner will still play a vital role deciding on features or trade-offs that need to be determined during the beta phase. You may, as part of your user testing, uncover new user needs that you weren't anticipating, and will need to make decisions on whether to incorporate these or not. Overall, this is a phase where a lot of software development should happen.

During this phase, using agile working practices (Chapter 4) will be paramount. Kanban should be your team's guide for what needs to get done in what sprint. It will also guide how to manage the backlog of requirements that will undoubtedly grow. Management of your software code will be critical, both in terms of access and for future-proofing. Using code repositories such as GitHub will allow your teams to work openly and productively. They should also use such repository and coding communities to avoid reinventing the wheel. If code can be taken from elsewhere that works and then built on (known as 'forking'), all the better.

Depending on your technology stack and organizational preferences, you may wish to share code back out in the open. Such 'open source' community approaches are highly commendable and are the foundations upon which the internet was built. In some scenarios, security or commercially sensitive issues may prevent you from sharing code, but if you can, do share.

You should be testing for all manner of concerns in beta. User testing should continue to pick up bugs or errors that have occurred. Having another software developer review code is highly recommended to provide quality assurance. Testing that your service works on the devices, technology and web browsers your users are going to use is of course essential. In addition, performance test checks should be run: how quickly the service runs is a key consideration. Sadly, attention spans are low and you are likely to lose customers if a web page or login doesn't progress within a few seconds (at most).

You will also need to proactively manage any code dependencies: are you reliant on code from third party providers, or data streams from them? Dependency management tools – which are typically bespoke to different programming languages – can help here, as these should automatically provide updates at key points in your software development lifecycle.

Security testing is clearly critical in this phase too. Penetration testing can help to assess how robust your service is from cyber attacks. Judgement will be required regarding how much mitigation and security is necessary. You should always do everything to protect your users' data and certain highly sensitive services may require additional levels of cybersecurity protection.

It's vital that your service doesn't exclude anyone accidentally. Key accessibility considerations include: colour blindness, hearing impairments or language challenges, although this is by no means a comprehensive list. Use the beta phase to give final assurance that accessibility has been designed into your service. We will cover more on this in Chapter 15.

By the end of this phase, you should have a working, functioning digital service that a decent volume of users is actively using. You're now ready to move into the live phase.

LIVE

The live phase is when your service is up, running and available to customers and users. Don't think the hard work stops here. You need to continuously update, upgrade and improve your service. This may be because you receive feedback from users about bugs or issues, or that software dependencies necessitate a change.

Using techniques such as DevOps can help in your live phase. This is a process that serves a dual function: ensuring the safe running and up-time of the service, and also deploying improvements at regular intervals. At heart, DevOps looks to bring together two potentially polarized sets of developer teams: those that have developed the service and those that look after its running. Together they should take responsibility for smooth running and continuous improvement.

Choosing when to deploy upgrades and improvements is tricky. If it necessitates your system to go down for a period of time, it's essential you forewarn users and mitigate any negative experiences they might encounter from this downtime.

RETIREMENT

Of course, everything has a retirement age. When your service no longer meets its intended user needs, or when something is ready to replace it, you need a plan for decommissioning. This should involve notifying users and helping them make any changes necessary to move to a new or alternative service. It will require protecting, storing and having a management plan for the data that has been accumulated as part of the running of the service. And it should mean that the retired service is no longer accessible.

Sharing knowledge

Creating digital services will leave you with a wealth of knowledge, experiences and lessons learned. It may also provide you with code that is valuable to others. You should also have learned new things about users and their preferences. Being open to sharing this with the wider development community helps make everyone's experiences better. At the bare minimum you should ensure your code, user research and reflections are shared within your organization. However, you may look to go further. Perhaps you've created new forms of data that might be valuable to others. Could these be made available by APIs or other forms of data transfer? Maybe a collaboration with another digital service could improve user experience even more. The world of platforms (Chapter 11) is built on the premise that sharing benefits everyone. It's a good principle to have in mind as you build your services.

Stage gates, assessments and pivots

During the design process, you may wish to use a stage gate at each phase as an opportunity to check in on progress. While it's not desirable to slow things down unnecessarily, building in some time to step back and check that things are progressing as intended can be beneficial. It also affords a very valuable opportunity: to cancel a project before it goes on too long, becomes too expensive or just outright fails. In the start-up world, this might be called an opportunity for a 'pivot'. Or it might just be a means of saving face.

Many digital governments across the world that use this design process use the end of each phase to provide an opportunity for 'service assessments'. These can help you understand if the development has gone as planned and is abiding by agreed principles. This may also be a neat approach to borrow for your organization, particularly if you're worried about lots of initiatives spiralling out of control.

Where next?

You may have decided to buy your technology. That's OK. The approaches set out in this chapter are still valuable. Ideally, your preferred supplier will work largely in line with them. Don't be afraid to have an open conversation with them about how they work; you may even be able to provide them with some advice or learn more about how they do things.

If you are going down the building route, always think of this as an experimental and iterative process. Every service built will teach you something new about your organization, your users and technology. Make sure you record, share and learn these lessons. Show-and-tells (Chapter 4) can be a great way of sharing knowledge, and you might look to book in a series of them to run alongside your service development.

If you are building services with a mixed economy method, make sure that the contractors, agencies and consultancies that you've been working alongside transfer their knowledge over to your teams before disbanding. You could even build this into their contracts from the offset, specifying requirements around skills transfer and sharing of code and documentation.

And finally, if you're reading this at a point where you've just retired a service, then celebrate. This represents a monumental achievement. Relax, enjoy yourself and reflect. This stuff isn't easy, so you deserve to have some fun.

BRINGING THE PRINCIPLE TO LIFE
How pivoting to building services in-house gave birth to an ecommerce giant

Shopify, the ecommerce marketplace, didn't begin life as Shopify as we know it. In fact, it wasn't even called Shopify. It was called Snowdevil and it started in 2004 as an online store that sold snowboards. From Snowdevil's perspective, it sold goods to customers. As such, it could have easily chosen to just use someone else's technology for ecommerce parts of fulfilling its user need: payments, notifications, confirmations and so on. But, with a programming expert as its founder, Tobias Lütke, it chose to build its own ecommerce software. And so a Canadian, and later global, legend was born.

Snowdevil's sales were fairly slow going, but enquiries came in from other online stores asking about its ecommerce capabilities. In 2006, the company pivoted into becoming an ecommerce platform for other online retailers, an offering it made open to other businesses in 2007. By 2009, over $100 million of sales passed through the Shopify platform. It subsequently expanded into many other software-as-a-service (see Chapter 11) capabilities that gave it a valuation of around $180 billion in 2020.

The critical point here is that while Shopify's – or Snowdevil's – initial ambitions to meet user needs failed, because it was in control of its technology destiny, it was able to pivot its offering to meet newly discovered user needs – namely, those of other businesses. Had it been reliant on an external software supplier for ecommerce functionality, such possibilities wouldn't have been open to it. Snowboards to multi-billion-dollar technology enterprises: facilitated by a simple decision to build in-house.[1]

Tips and tricks

- Share the agile project management approach widely with stakeholders. This will get them comfortable with what you're trying to do, and how. Hopefully they'll be left with no surprises.

- Book in 'rituals' as calendar meetings to reinforce the approach. This will help you to stay honest and run agile daily stand-ups, weekly or bi-weekly sprint planning, retrospectives, and end-of-phase show-and-tells. This will help cement the rhythm of your ways of working.

- Find and cultivate digital specialists that you want to work with. They are in demand, so it's as much as selling what you're doing to them as paying them to just do a job. Ask around and, if necessary, consider using well-regarded digital recruiters.

- Work out which communities of practice you should engage with. This will probably be best informed by the technology stack you're working with. If you're using open-source technologies, these should come with a wide and vibrant community of practice. You should find insights, lessons learned and potentially code-sharing are all real benefits from this.

- Keep an eye on the benefits. In the discovery phase you should identify the likely end benefits from your service development. Iterate and refresh these as you go. You don't want to get to the end of a beta only to be blocked in your progress because your senior stakeholders were expecting different benefits from the ones you're now likely to deliver.

What you might say in your next meeting

By building digital service in-house, we'll be taking back control from big suppliers.

Software development is expensive; this methodology will help us de-risk the process and should reduce costs.

Who's done something similar? Can we adapt their codebase?

It's OK to call it a day at the end of a phase. It's better to fail cheaply and quickly rather than slowly and expensively.

Open source benefits everyone.

Where you can find out more

For a great exposition of the importance of good service design and some great examples, Lou Downe, former head of design of the UK Government Digital Service, has written *Good Services: How to design services that work* (BIS Publishers, 2020). In addition, Andrew Greenway, an early founder member of the Government Digital Service, has articulated the digital unit's key lessons – and in particular the importance of building great digital services in-house – in *Digital Transformation at Scale: Why the strategy is delivery* (London Publishing Partnership, 2018).

Note

1 For more on the Shopify story, read: Entrepreneur Europe (2018) 5 big brands that had massively successful pivots, 15 February, www.entrepreneur.com/article/308975 (archived at https://perma.cc/S5KJ-KJKA)

10

Buying technology

Let's avoid one of the most expensive mistakes you could ever make.

The principle in a nutshell

Failed IT procurements have derailed many promising careers. Fortunately for you, there's consequently a wealth of experience to rely upon to know what not to do.

Given the increasing commodification of so much technology since the 2000s, it's impossible to digitally transform an organization without buying something from somewhere. Luckily, many of the rules of good procurement of any goods and services apply to technology: only buying what you need; testing the market well; keeping a close relationship with suppliers. However, procuring digital offerings does require a few issues to be particularly mindful of. First, do not outsource to an external technology provider something that is truly core to your business: one of its 'core competencies'. Second, factor in the full lifecycle cost of a product or service. Remember that you may need upgrades, additional licences, service support and so forth. Third, take every case study shown to you with a pinch of salt. How well a technology operates in your organization is most likely a function of your organization. Just because someone else has achieved benefits doesn't necessarily mean you will too.

What's the problem being addressed?

Good procurement should help you:

- *Get what you actually need:* only buy to serve user needs, rather than what a technology salesperson is desperate to sell you. Procurement should be entirely led by user needs. Just like with building services, if you don't have a clear sense of what the use cases are, you risk buying the wrong thing.

- *Achieve best value:* value is about quality as well as price. Effective procurement should avoid you focusing purely on cost at the expense of all else. If something is suspiciously cheap, that's probably a warning sign.

- *Avoid supplier lock-in:* many technology contracts are multi-year. This is often for good reason – the longer the contract, the more certainty the supplier has, and – hopefully – this will translate to lower costs for you. But you don't want to be in a position where you are entirely beholden to a single supplier with no hope of ever escaping if something goes wrong, or if you simply wish to change supplier.

- *Understand full lifecycle costs:* good buying involves thinking ahead. How long will you need something for? For how many users? Might this rapidly scale up? Will you need to operate in new territories during the life of the contract? All of these things, and more, can lead to significant cost increases that aren't immediately obvious at the time of purchase. Forewarned is forearmed.

- *Manage suppliers effectively:* remember that you are the customer and you should expect good service. Tricky conversations may arise at times where you feel you are not being served as you expected or wished. Good procurement and contracting should give you the ability to manage – and, if necessary, negotiate with – your suppliers in an evidence-based way to help you achieve the outcomes you expect.

Putting the principle into action

Be clear on the user needs

You won't be surprised to know that before buying anything, you should be crystal clear on your user needs. Who is this for? What do they require from the technology? Understanding these questions will allow you to specify your user requirements. This allows you to focus on what you really need, potentially saving money in the process. You don't want to be in a position where you're buying a technology without being clear on the why. A common example is organizations buying customer relationship management (CRM) platforms. These can be hugely powerful, particularly for organizations with high volumes of customers who need regular contact. However, given the wide *potential* functionality of CRMs – from sales to marketing to compliance and more – often organizations buy CRMs without a well-defined user need, assuming that it's just a 'good thing to do'. In practice, disappointment often abounds: according to one *Harvard Business Review* article in 2018, 90 per cent of executives felt their CRM systems had failed to help their businesses grow.[1]

To build or to buy

In Chapter 9 we covered when and where to build digital services. Figure 10.1 outlines a number of considerations for whether to build or buy, depending on the nature of purchase. Whether something is a 'core competency' refers to whether it is central to the value proposition of your entity in the eyes of your customer. If it is a 'novel technology', it's something new or still in its infancy. 'Commodity technology', by contrast, is long established. Essentially, you should seek to buy non-core competencies (such as cloud hosting), build novel core competencies (such as machine learning software, if you are an AI company), avoid any novel technologies that are non-core (because this just puts risks into your organization) and reconsider whether you need to customize or make proprietary any core competencies that are effectively just commodity technology.

Move away from legacy technology

Legacy technology is a catch-all term that refers to technology, systems, software and hardware that are still in use by an organization yet have become obsolete. In other words, the suppliers or vendors of the technology no

FIGURE 10.1 Build versus buy considerations

Core competency	**Build**	**Reconsider**
Non-core competency	**Avoid**	**Buy**
	Novel technology	Commodity technology

longer provide upgrades or services to it. This is a nightmare position. If the technology – which can cover anything from back-office processes to front-of-house customer services – is still used by the organization, this leaves the organization highly vulnerable and exposed. Any future changes are likely to be extremely costly, relying on scarce resources; invariably these are freelance contractors or external specialists. And the legacy technology acts as a lowest common denominator for the organization. Any attempts to build new services on the technology risk perpetuating the lock-in, and so workarounds or duplicative data transfers end up being required. At all possible opportunities, look to avoid buying technologies coming close to the end of their lifecycle or switch suppliers before it's too late.

Explore the landscape

Once you understand what you're trying to buy, you should explore the technology landscape. You emphatically should *not* just buy the first thing that you stumble upon. While you don't want to overdo efforts – particularly if the value is low – you should always be looking to evaluate suppliers and offers against each other. Exploration requires imagination. Of course, internet searches are a good first start, but remember wise suppliers will be using online advertising, paid magazine advertorials and all manner of techniques to sell their wares to you. So treat everything you read with a critical eye. Ask trusted peers in other companies for their honest views about potential products. If you're a member of a trade association or industry body, they may be able to provide a confidential forum for sharing knowledge and experiences.

Test where possible

To give yourself the best opportunity of a successful procurement, just like when building services, prototype. Develop a simple prototype to allow you to understand how the technology you're aiming to buy will affect your business processes. This should allow you to see if you've missed anything in your user requirements, or whether unexpected issues might arise. For instance, if you're looking to invest in a robotic process automation technology, such as that pioneered by UiPath, develop a very simple worked example. This could be as rudimentary as Post-It notes that specify the datasets to be integrated and the data that is intended to flow across systems.

By doing so, you'll get a sense of the scale of the operations and the required linkages. By making the future state 'real', you'll be in a better position when it comes to buying.

And of course, if you can, test your prototype with real users. What have they learned from the test experience? How does it meet the desired outcomes you're seeking to achieve from the procurement? All of this needs to feed into your thinking and, if necessary, cause you to iterate your requirements.

Integrate with your technology stack

Reflect on your technology stack, which we covered in Chapter 8. How will what you're buying affect it? Does the product rely on data feeds from existing parts of your stack? How easy will those be to enable? Since the mid-2010s, most major suppliers have become acutely aware of the importance of interoperability – usually enabled through APIs – within technology systems. These are likely to be critical in enabling the smooth transfer of information between your systems.

Building from existing technologies might also be a way to achieve better value. Many major cloud host providers – Microsoft Azure, AWS, Google and so forth – build additional products on top of their cloud facilities. If you are an existing customer, it may be that you are able to access these products at a better rate, and that they cover the functionality you're after while reducing any integration costs.

As you look to buy technology, always look to the future. How will you manage a major strategic change of direction in your business that requires a tech overhaul? Will it be possible to exit or ramp down usage of certain contracts easily? How easily can you switch providers? The answer to this question will be dependent on the nature of the market: if there is only one provider for the solution you are after, your ability to switch will be severely constrained. As such, you may wish to disaggregate parts of the solution as much as possible, so that you are not reliant on one, large supplier. This brings significant risks to the business: what if the supplier fails, performs poorly, or moves its product portfolio away from that which you've bought? These are some of the reasons why – if appropriate – open-source technologies are highly popular – because they rely on large communities of practice rather than small, closed developer supplier teams in order to survive and thrive.

Do the business case

In Chapter 6 we covered the importance of funding to successful digital endeavours. Suffice to say, do a business case, and do it well. Understanding the costs of what you're aiming to buy is critical. Within this, make sure to differentiate between:

- upfront/implementation costs;
- licence fees;
- ongoing run costs;
- configuration changes;
- any other potential current or future costs;

This will require detailed investigations and conversations with potential suppliers. While upfront costs and licence fees should be relatively easy to source, ongoing or configuration changes may only become apparent once you have really thought about how this technology will change your business. Ongoing costs can cover everything from upgrades and patches to service management charges, such as call centres to help your staff if something goes wrong. Configuration changes might be incurred if you need the software to be customized to your specific business needs. Under all scenarios, the longer you have the software and hardware, and the greater the number of users, the higher the costs. So be realistic and pessimistic when you consider the full lifecycle costs – better to overestimate than underestimate.

Don't buy in haste to repent at leisure

What constitutes a 'big' purchase will vary depending on the size of your organization. Notwithstanding, as a rule of thumb, anything that constitutes over 5 per cent of your annual digital budget should certainly fall under that category. And if your organization is of a multi-billion scale, probably 2 per cent is a better guide. For such major purchases, you should follow all procurement best practice.

Do pre-market engagement. Either use an established framework or reach out to potential suppliers to invite them to showcase their products to you. Ask for their feedback on what you're aiming to achieve through both the purchase and ultimate outcomes you're seeking to deliver. There is a common misconception that this would prejudice any procurement outcomes. Of course, consult any relevant in-house legal and procurement teams to ensure you are fully compliant with national, international and sector laws and regulations. But generally speaking, it is highly advisable to conduct pre-market engagement. It enables you to know the market better, and for your potential suppliers to understand your needs better.

While you're meeting with suppliers, always be discerning when reviewing case studies they send you. One piece of HR software in one organization may have helped deliver 30 per cent efficiencies, but that's no guarantee – unless you specify it in the contract – that this will be achievable in your organization. Always read the small print about timescales as well: were improvements sustained? Most suppliers will engage in product demonstrations. During such demonstrations, make sure to understand the difference between prototypes and fully operational products. Ask how many instances of the technology have been implemented, what versions have been implemented, and how they are performing.

Most larger organizations will have procurement teams. If you don't, consider reaching out to a procurement specialist to help develop your process for you. The critical thing is to establish your requirements, your evaluation criteria for suppliers, and the process you will follow for the evaluation. Once you've done this, it's vital you follow the process as you originally set out. Otherwise, you may be at risk of a legal challenge that the procurement was unfair or discriminatory. Again, your procurement teams or advisers can help you avoid this scenario.

When establishing evaluation criteria, you will wish to consider factors along the lines of:

- *Strategic fit:* how does this align with the wider objectives of your organization?
- *Quality:* how well does the technology perform?
- *Price:* how do the full lifecycle costs compare between options?
- *Risk:* how much risk does this leave your organization exposed to (eg potential vendor lock-in)?

Your evaluation process should be formally recorded with a clear audit trail. Once you have a preferred supplier, you should notify them and can begin conversations to develop and then finalize contractual arrangements.

Contract management and outcomes versus outputs versus inputs

One of the most critical issues to cover in contracts is, 'what does success look like?' It's important to articulate and specify this in measurable terms. By putting this into the contract with your supplier, you can manage their performance to ensure they deliver on these measures. Success could be constituted as:

- **Outcomes:** the technology helps to deliver a given outcome metric (eg financial efficiency).
- **Outputs:** the technology has led to a specific change (eg number of new users).
- **Inputs:** the technology supplier has provided a series of measurable things (eg number of person days provided).

You should consider which metric, or a blend of metrics, to apply depending on your specific circumstances. It's useful to think of these metrics as a means of transferring risk from buyer to supplier, or vice versa. For instance, a sales and marketing programme looking to procure an outsourced digital marketing solution may wish to major on outcome metrics from their supplier. The supplier may reasonably look to charge a premium in doing so, because the risk is transferred onto them. Achieving outcomes such as improved revenue may be dependent on factors beyond the immediate remit of the digital marketing provider, and so this presents a risk to the supplier. Similarly, input metrics largely remove risk from the supplier. A supplier that provides 300 days of technology resources to build a piece of software has no liability in the contract beyond ensuring that the days are provided as specified in the contract. This would be a simple contract to manage, but one where the risk for the software being a success lies almost entirely on the buyer.

Manage the relationship strategically

You have broadly two ways to manage your suppliers: transactionally or like a partnership. The first instance makes most sense if you are buying simple commodity products and can easily switch suppliers if desired. In this scenario, you should constantly keep an eye on the critical terms of your contract and ensure that the supplier is delivering value against the contracted terms. If not, you should be in a position to refer back to your specified requirements and be in a strong position to seek improvements (either in service delivery or potentially invoking financial penalties) from the supplier.

The partnership relationship is wise if you are highly dependent on a supplier for a critical function in your organization and have limited opportunities to switch suppliers. This is known as a 'strategic supplier'. Here, you should consider the supplier as a partner – engaging frequently and exploring avenues for mutual benefit. For example, an insurance brokerage for a niche market may be heavily reliant on a bespoke software supplier for its case management function. In this instance, the relationship is important to both parties. It may be possible to explore how the supplier could develop new products in line with the needs of the buyer. This would benefit the customer organization and the supplier, and represent strong partnership working.

Keep an eye out for contract expiry

Nothing lasts forever. Every contract has an expiry period. You don't want to be facing a cliff edge when yours approaches; this will leave you in a weak negotiating position. Keep a log of all major contracts and expiry dates or review points, and systematically go through and assess what action is needed when. Rolling over contracts may be the easiest option, but it may not provide best value. And if you're intending on changing a supplier, as we have just learned, this requires careful planning and advanced thinking.

Where next?

Good buying takes time. Map out the critical stakeholders you need to engage in the process. Who will ultimately sign off on the decision? Where does the funding come from? Who needs to be part of the evaluation? Work with your procurement colleagues to set up a clear process and deadline for a decision. Once you've made a decision, it's essential that you don't consider this the end of the process. Getting a good contract in place requires careful attention. Don't just accept whatever boilerplate contracts already exist. Tailor as necessary to your needs and situation.

Even when you've got a new supplier on board, don't think you need to be 'exclusive' in your relationship. It's always sensible to scan the market. Assess what competitors are doing and, if new entrants are arriving, how they compare with what you have. By always being abreast of new developments, you'll be in a stronger position to know whether you need to think about changing suppliers or renegotiating terms with them when their contract is up.

BRINGING THE PRINCIPLE TO LIFE
The case of Hertz, Accenture, digital transformation and a $32 million lawsuit

In April 2019, Hertz, the automotive rental giant, filed a $32 million lawsuit against the global technology and advisory firm, Accenture. Hertz, in its filing, claimed Accenture's work was 'deficient in multiple respects'. Citing a failure to 'develop a responsive website' and 'deficient' programming, Hertz sought to recoup the advisory fees it had paid Accenture during 2016 and 2017, as part of its wider $400 million digital transformation agenda.

Owing to Hertz's filing of bankruptcy in late 2020, it is not possible to draw full conclusions from this unsavoury relationship, as the lawsuit stalled. However, a few observations do stand out from the lawsuit filing regarding technology procurement. First, as Hertz aimed to regain its edge against more digitally advanced competitors such as Avis, it embarked on an ambitious digital transformation programme. In doing so, it aimed to make a digital customer experience part of its core value proposition. Yet it chose the dangerous route of relying on external suppliers to do so. As the company stated in its filing: 'Hertz did not have the internal expertise or resources to execute such a massive undertaking; it needed to partner with a world-class technology services firm.' As a result, it outsourced one of its potential future core competencies – always a potential risk. Second, Hertz chose Accenture after 'an impressive, one-day presentation'. While we cannot be certain this was the only supplier engagement made with Accenture prior to contract award, if this had been the case, it would be unlikely to give as full assurance as ideal. And finally, Hertz did not appear to engage in significant prototyping prior to procurement. As the filing noted, the 'design, build, test and deploy' of Hertz's 'new website and mobile applications' was all reliant on Accenture.[2]

Sadly, such stories of digital procurements gone awry are not uncommon and history would indicate the blame is never simple to apportion. Yet the case study of Hertz and Accenture points to a few areas where better buying practices of technology might have helped.

Tips and tricks

- Focus on the user needs and ultimate business transformation you're trying to achieve. Let these guide your procurement, not the technology solutions.
- Who do you trust to give you good, impartial advice on potential providers? Reach out to your network. In addition, consider if your company has non-executive board members or advisers who might be able to help.
- Don't be seduced by snappy presentations and demonstrations. Try and think: 'how will this actually work in my organization?'
- Establish a clear governance process for the procurement. Involve senior members in the organization as necessary.
- Cast a critical eye on the benefits suggested by suppliers. If you were to apply optimism bias to these, how would it affect the benefits case?

What you might say in your next meeting

We're entering into a long-term relationship with this supplier. Let's make sure we both benefit from it.

We need to invite a variety and range of suppliers to our pre-market engagement.

What are the metrics we are going to use to evaluate whether this has been a success or not?

Record all contract discussions. You never know when we might need this information.

Cheapest isn't necessarily best.

Where you can find out more

For more eye-opening stories of procurements gone wrong – and, more positively, procurement sometimes gone *right* – as well as some practical advice and guidance, read Peter Smith's *Bad Buying: How organizations waste billions, through failures, fraud and f*ck ups* (Penguin Business, 2020).

Notes

1 Edinger, S (2018) Why CRM projects fail and how to make them more
   successful, *Harvard Business Review*, 20 December, hbr.org/2018/12/why-crm-
   projects-fail-and-how-to-make-them-more-successful (archived at https://perma.
   cc/9WH6-YXXU)
2 Information from: *The Hertz Corporation v Accenture LLP* from the United
   States District Court Southern District of New York (2019) , filed 19 April,
   regmedia.co.uk/2019/04/23/hertz-accenture-website.pdf (archived at https://
   perma.cc/JU2Q-EUBQ)

11

The cloud, APIs and open source

Work out how your digital transformation fits into the wider ecosystem of the internet.

The principle in a nutshell

One of the hardest parts of the job of a digital leader is to separate the signal from the noise when it comes to trends in digital transformation. Three particular, and related, trends have become dominant since the 2000s which are all unified by the concept of sharing: the cloud; application program interfaces; and open-source technologies.

Each of these presents major considerations and implications for any organization. What responsibilities lie with your enterprise or third parties? How do you build upon the data and services provided by entities outside of your company? Should you contribute to data flows in your wider industry? And what role do you aim to play in technology developments more generally? By proactively considering your cloud, API and open-source strategies, you will be best placed to answer all of these questions in a manner that suits your overall aims.

What's the problem being addressed?

The era of digital is powered by the internet. While so many technologies that the internet affords may seem ethereal and almost magical, the internet itself is an extremely physical, tactile phenomenon. It is, quite simply, hundreds of thousands of miles of cables – hundreds of which sit at the bottom of the sea – that carry information which connects, via satellites, Wi-Fi, routers, servers and data centres, computer networks together.

It is this transfer and connection of data that presents so many technological possibilities. Three in particular are fundamental bedrock considerations for any digital transformation programme:

- *Cloud computing:* essentially, where and how data that pertains to an organization is stored and accessed. The rise of cloud computing has been one of the biggest reasons for the vast expanse in data capture and related possibilities of AI, data science and machine learning.

- *APIs:* a popular mode of exposing or sharing valuable information from one application to another, upon which multiple, nimble services ('microservices') may be developed.

- *Open source:* an approach to software licensing – effectively, permitting someone to use software – which allows users of the software to edit, modify, adapt or distribute the software without incurring a licence fee or charge.

Your approach to each of these could radically change your overall digital transformation, for better or worse.

Putting the principle into action

What the cloud enables: the 'as-a-service' menu of options

Proto incarnations of the internet emerged in the late 1960s as the US Department of Defense's Advanced Research Projects Agency Network (ARPANET) created a network that connected computers via a transmission control protocol/internet protocol (TCP/IP), allowing them to share resources and information. Over time, three particular features emerged that built on such connections that made what we know today as *cloud computing* possible: the development of specific services such as the storing of data; sharing of resources across multiple users, known as 'virtualization'; and the enablement of access to these services by different users, known as 'networking'.[1]

These building blocks were capitalized upon by Amazon Web Services in the early 2000s, which led to the creation of 'public cloud' services. In the cloud, companies could access storage, maintenance and hosting facilities all managed by Amazon (or future cloud providers), thereby removing the need to have such expensive hardware on site (also known as 'on premise').

Since the 2010s, the power of cloud computing has allowed companies to significantly reduce their technology and hardware costs, and potentially scale and expand their services and offerings in a way that would have been prohibitively expensive in the pre-cloud era.

In Chapter 8 we touched upon some high-level technology stack considerations. Cloud computing allows you to flex provision of different elements of your stack to meet your business and wider aims. Four potential models of using the cloud should be considered as part of your digital transformation plans, derived from a model developed by the website Hosting Advice (Table 11.1).[2]

TABLE 11.1   Relationship between technical layers and cloud computing options

Technical layers		Cloud options			
Stack component	Description	On-premises	Infrastructure-as-a-service (IaaS)	Platform-as-a-service (PaaS)	Software-as-a-service (SaaS)
Applications	Software configured to perform specific tasks	You manage	You manage	You manage	Others manage
Data	Information that flows across layers to facilitate use of applications	You manage	You manage	You manage	Others manage
Middleware	Software that sits between and connects applications and operating systems, an example of which is security authentication	You manage	You manage	Others manage	Others manage
Operating system(s)	Software that manages computer hardware to create usable services	You manage	You manage	Others manage	Others manage

(continued)

TABLE 11.1   (Continued)

Technical layers		Cloud options			
Stack component	Description	On-premises	Infrastructure-as-a-service (IaaS)	Platform-as-a-service (PaaS)	Software-as-a-service (SaaS)
Virtualization	Creation of abstraction layers that separate out key parts of hardware that can be accessed virtually	You manage	Others manage	Others manage	Others manage
Servers	Collection and dissemination of information across a network	You manage	Others manage	Others manage	Others manage
Storage	Retention – permanently or temporarily – of data	You manage	Others manage	Others manage	Others manage
Networking	Computers or devices that are connected together	You manage	Others manage	Others manage	Others manage

ON-PREMISES

In this option, the full list of layers outlined in Table 11.1 reside on your business site. These will require upkeep, maintenance, appropriate storage facilities and estate costs, at least. Servers are getting smaller all the time, but air-conditioned server rooms – owing to the heat emitted from processing – are still likely to be necessary. In this model, all the risk, cost and responsibility lie with your organization. This gives you the most control, but potentially the most headaches.

INFRASTRUCTURE-AS-A-SERVICE (IAAS)

Under an IaaS model, you should have all of the functionality of on-premises without the requirement to physically store, maintain and manage the hardware. You can of course still access all your servers, storage, networking and virtualization layer; however, this is done – usually via APIs – through a connection to the 'virtual cloud'. The term itself is a bit misleading – there are no clouds, just large data server farms dotted across the world. But the point is you can access them from wherever.

IaaS models do require clients to manage operating systems, middleware, data and applications. This model is particularly attractive to companies looking to rapidly scale up their offerings (and thus need flexibility in increasing storage) and companies that desire a fair amount of control over their technical layers. Clients will be dependent on IaaS providers for security and may find that certain older systems are not supported in these cloud environments. Amazon Elastic Compute Cloud (EC2) or Microsoft Azure are popular examples of IaaS.

PLATFORM-AS-A-SERVICE (PAAS)

Companies going down the PaaS route cede more control over their technical layers, instead only managing applications and data. PaaS customers tend to be software developers. The PaaS model allows developers to focus on their core business of software creation, without concerning themselves too much with storage, infrastructure or operating systems.

PaaS is perfect for organizations seeking to build new and bespoke software. It tends to be simple, relatively cost-effective and easily scalable. Should a new start-up operating a PaaS model suddenly experience a surge of new customers, and thus storage requirements, it will be simple to flex up storage as needed.

Owing to the reliance of the PaaS model on other providers for much of the technical layers, this can create challenges of interoperability. If PaaS relies on accessing data or information from a legacy system that is not supported in the cloud, this is likely to be problematic. PaaS may also create lock-in scenarios, where an organization finds itself reliant on the PaaS provider going forward.

AWS Elastic Beanstalk is a good example of the PaaS model, whereby over 100 distinct services are made available to developers, and environments where code can be deployed and applications built are easily supported.

SOFTWARE-AS-A-SERVICE (SAAS)

SaaS involves buying software and using it over the internet. It removes the need for programs to be installed and run locally on devices; it's all done in the cloud. This is the most flexible model and, according to the research firm 451, by 2018, over a quarter of enterprises ran workflows – business processes, in other terms – using SaaS models.[3]

Companies have no responsibility for maintenance, hardware or software updates under this model. Monthly subscriptions are usually required for use, with popular examples being Dropbox or Google Workspace (which includes Google Docs, Sheets, Drive and so forth).

While this model offers the greatest ease of use, it is the least flexible; organizations are entirely reliant on the SaaS provider for security or downtime issues, and have no or limited ability to customize features. That said, it is a highly powerful model and one which many organizations are opting for to provide services which are not core to their business, but essential for their operations.

Making sense of it all: a floral example

So what does this mean for your business? Effectively, cloud computing grants you a menu of options from which to trade off cost, risk and functionality. As always, you should be guided by user needs: what is your business actually about, what do customers truly value, and thus what do you need to have control over? Consider a simple analogy. Let's say you want to go into the flower business. The layers required to run this business will cover everything from how a customer buys the flower through to the vehicle needed to transport goods across your supply chain through to the fields where flowers are actually grown. You may not necessarily want to be responsible – or pay – for all of these layers. The *type* of flower business you run should guide your cloud choice. A flower maker and seller would probably aim to control as many of its layers as possible: the on-premises model. A company that lets customers buy flowers but arranges the flowers themselves might go for more of an IaaS model. A company that provides subscription letter-box flowers, such as Bloom & Wild or Freddie's Flower, might go for an analogous PaaS model. And a company that sends flowers to someone who buys them via an online broker – effectively matching demand to supply – would probably be more akin to a SaaS model.

Standing on shoulders through using APIs

Ever wondered how you can access BBC News through your Amazon Alexa? Or how your Spotify playlist connects seamlessly while you're travelling in an Uber? The answer is via application program interfaces – APIs.

APIs are the ultimate friends of software developers, allowing them to connect different programs together to the benefit of consumers.

According to the consultancy McKinsey, around $1 trillion of value – nearly half the size of the UK economy – could be added to the global economy if companies shared information even better via APIs.[4] While APIs are a beautifully simple concept, managing your API strategy requires a deep understanding of your business objectives, end-user needs and financial planning.

The transfer of information via APIs can be accomplished in a number of ways. Unless you are a software developer yourself, you don't need to know exactly *how to do this*, but as a digital lead it's essential you understand the fundamentals of *how it's done*. These means, depending on the nature of information being transferred, can include:

- *Unique Reference Locators (URLs):* whereby a web browser accesses a web resource (often a website) which is located on a computer network;

- *HyperText Transport Protocol (HTTP)* (now usually HTTPS), which is a web-based means whereby a *client*, via a web browser, makes a request to a *server* (or application running on the internet) and the *server* returns the information such as HTML or file;

- *JavaScript Object Notation (JSON):* a popular and simple means of transferring data between *client* and *server*, using a standardized format that is common to all programming languages;

- *Comma Separated Values (CSVs):* which remain extremely common, and use tabular spreadsheets to structure and provide information. While these can lead to error – often due to a lack of consistency in how data is structured in them – they are popular as they provide a simple and flexible way for analysts to access data.[5]

You need to consider APIs in two ways: as a potential consumer and as a provider. For the former, ensure your development teams are fully sighted on the potential for APIs to improve business flows. They should – as part of the service design work we covered in Chapter 9 – proactively consider what information would improve user experience, and where APIs could enhance this experience. You will also need to address the potential financial implications of accessing someone's APIs. If it's not free, you need to understand the cost implications and how these may change over time and with demand.

As a provider of APIs, you similarly need to have a proper strategy in place. How could enabling APIs to be accessed by other entities benefit your consumers and organization? The food sharing platform, Deliveroo, has APIs which facilitate 'point of sale' integration between restaurateurs. The easier Deliveroo makes it for restaurants to join the platform, the better it is for their users. Of course, creating, curating and maintaining APIs requires developer resources. How should this be paid for? Typical models include:

- *pay per use:* with a payment made per transaction;
- *revenue share:* where companies may share (not necessarily equally) customers' revenues; and
- *free:* which makes most sense if the creator of the API benefits from as many integrated partners as possible.

APIs provide an opportunity to offer an integrated experience for your users, which could deliver significant financial benefits to your organization as well. Any good digital transformation plan should have them at the heart of its thinking.

Benefits and pitfalls of open source

While APIs and open source both share a common philosophy of making things open, they are not the same thing. APIs may be open and freely available, but they may also come at a cost. Open source, by contrast, is based on the principle that the ability to use, edit and update software should be totally free. A typical software vendor operating in a 'closed-source software development model' would charge a fee for implementation and costs for licences. Only a defined number of developers would be allowed to access the source code and work on it. Open source means making the source code freely available for any developer to work on.

Open-source software requires resourcing in terms of software development – and these will be required through the lifecycle of the software, as it is upgraded and improved – but there will never be a licence fee.

In your digital transformation, you should have the option for open-source software in your potential list of options when acquiring new technology. There are obvious benefits to open source: you are in control of edits and modifications, which is particularly important if your business needs change; costs will likely be lower than closed-source models; and ultimately, you are in greater control of your technological destiny. However, do not confuse freely available with free. Depending on the open-source technology – the operating systems Linux and Android are some of the most commonly known ones – developers familiar with the code base may be a rare commodity, and thus expensive. And another important consideration is how you evaluate open-source software. With closed-source software you are evaluating for track record, cost and the type of relationship you foresee with the vendor. In an open-source model, pay close attention to the open-source developer community. How much have they released? How large and active is the community? What industry standards – such as ISO27001 or Cloud Security Principles – does the community abide by?

Where next?

What we've covered in this chapter may seem initially quite technical, but as we've discovered, these topics can have a material impact on your overall business. It's important therefore to factor in issues such as cloud strategies, APIs and whether or not to pursue open-source technologies in your thinking. Don't just leave such considerations to your technical teams. If your organization typically delegates such technical architecture questions to the 'IT team', make sure you get to know them and interrogate their thinking. Remember: cloud can give you scale and flexibility while saving money; APIs can allow you to build in new features and services from other companies, to the benefit of your customers; and open-source technologies could eradicate licence fees and put you in charge of your overall technical destiny.

BRINGING THE PRINCIPLE TO LIFE
Tracking the rise of the technology giants

What links Amazon, Microsoft, Google, Apple and Facebook? Beyond the obvious point that they are wildly successful and highly valued technology behemoths, it's critical to note that a key part of their business model in the 2020s was their *platform approach*, defined helpfully by Feng Zhu and Nathan Furr of Harvard Business School and INSEAD, 'as intermediaries that connect two or more distinct groups of users and enable their direct interaction'. Yet none of these companies started out as platforms.[6]

Amazon was initially a retailer, pivoting in 2000 to becoming a marketplace and later launching AWS. Google's search engine functionality would become a highly integrated advertising giant. And Apple majored on products such as the iPod before developing the App Store in 2008. All of these changes were enabled by API-based approaches allowing other businesses and developers to build on their offerings.

The Apple iOS operating system is a perfect case study of how opening up a previously highly closed system to developers delivered huge benefits to both Apple users and the company itself. The Apple Software Development Kit (SDK) was launched in March 2008 and enabled developers to create apps exclusively for Apple devices. According to Statista, the market research company, as of June 2017, 180 billion Apple App Store apps had been downloaded.

Such benefits haven't just been confined to the technology world. The travel website Expedia receives an estimated 90 per cent of its total revenues ($12 billion in 2019) through APIs. By allowing third parties to integrate into its platform, customers can easily book cars, hotels, flights and more. In return, Expedia takes a fee for allowing this interoperability. Of course, the power of the platform model is that the benefits may be shared; customers benefit from a simplified experience (rather than having to handle multiple searches and booking), the third-party providers receive income from customers, and of course Expedia benefits too through more customers and more revenue.[7]

Tips and tricks

- The terminology of 'the cloud' may seem mystical but don't let it fool or intimidate you. The magic of the internet is based on as much the physical that you can see and touch as the digital that you experience through software applications.

- To get a handle of what's going on in your organization, map out the current state. It's likely going to be a bit messy; certain services or products may use a hybrid of open source, closed source, some APIs and some cloud or not. But only by understanding the current state can you see what options you have to improve it.

- Look at your competitors and new entrants in your market. What choices are they making around the cloud and interoperability?

- If you're considering open-source approaches, make sure to familiarize yourself with the different open-source communities first. It may seem obvious, but the internet really is your best friend in terms of keeping up to speed with changing trends. Sites like the World Wide Web Consortium (W3) are a great resource here.

- If you're just starting out or have the benefit of a 'greenfield' technological landscape, check out OpenStack for a popular open-source platform.

What you might say in your next meeting

Where is our data held? If it's on our own premises, is that wise?

Who's in charge of our cloud strategy in this organization?

The more we share and borrow code or information from others, the better we can make the experience for our customers.

Do we have the digital capabilities in this organization to be an open-source company?

We don't need to call up Amazon when we're getting additional storage, so why should our customers need to call us up to access something from us? Can't we enable this through an API?

Where you can find out more

The internet really is the best place to keep on learning and finding out more. W3 is a great repository of information, but it's also just wise to visit developer communities and read their 'wikis' to learn more about what they do. Consultancies and companies provide great explainer blogs, although always remember that they are probably trying to sell you something, so work out what it is before reading. For a fascinating and practical guide to how platform approaches can transform government services, visit the website of Richard Pope, a senior fellow at the Harvard Kennedy School DigitalHKS Centre, for his guide to government platforms, 'Platformland': www.platformland.org

Notes

1 BCS: The Chartered Institute for IT blog (2019) History of the cloud, 19 March, www.bcs.org/content-hub/history-of-the-cloud/ (archived at https://perma.cc/ V5Z4-4FSK)

2 Hosting Advice website, www.hostingadvice.com/ (archived at https://perma. cc/2LX8-37WE)

3 451 Research blog (2016) Enterprise IT executives expect 60% of workloads will be run in the cloud by 2018, 1 September, 451research.com/blog/764-enterprise-it-executives-expect-60-of-workloads-will-run-in-the-cloud-by-2018?_ga=2.125060426.1906964010.1620314277-1678497958.1620133003 (archived at https://perma.cc/AP32-PPML)

4 McKinsey Digital blog (2017) What it really takes to capture the value of APIs, 12 September, www.mckinsey.com/business-functions/mckinsey-digital/our-insights/what-it-really-takes-to-capture-the-value-of-apis (archived at https://perma.cc/E5BF-RXKA)

5 UK Government Digital Service blog (2016) Our approach to APIs: the basics, 20 June, technology.blog.gov.uk/2016/06/20/our-approach-to-apis-the-basics/ (archived at https://perma.cc/RH4A-98ZG)

6 Zhu, F and Furr, N (2016) Products to platforms: making the leap, *Harvard Business Review*, hbr.org/2016/04/products-to-platforms-making-the-leap (archived at https://perma.cc/ULA5-KSC7)

7 Sharma, V (2017) What is driving the API economy growth?, USC Marshall blog, 10 October, www.marshall.usc.edu/blog/what-driving-api-economy-growth (archived at https://perma.cc/YH2G-J8Q3)

12

Using data science to inform decision-making

You should worry less about general artificial intelligence and more about how data can help you make better decisions.

The principle in a nutshell

Popular narratives of the future of digital transformation commonly focus on things such as autonomous robots, human-level artificial intelligence and machine learning. Yet before jumping to conclusions about how such exciting developments as these can fit into your future workplace, it's important to understand what makes them possible: data, and the use of data in a manner that can realize its potential.

The term 'data science' is a powerful umbrella description that – in the words of the computer scientists John D. Kelleher and Brendan Tierney – covers a 'set of principles, problem definitions, algorithms, and processes for extracting non-obvious and useful patterns from large data sets'.[1] It is the data science approach that affords so many possibilities ahead of us: from Google advertising recommendations to facial recognition software. However, before we get easily distracted by a vision of robots taking everyone's jobs, let's first focus on how data science makes such a vision even possible, and what the strengths, weaknesses and implications of data science are.

What's the problem being addressed?

Data science, and its cousin artificial intelligence, has been popular many times over.[2] The swell of interest that emerged in the mid-2000s was preceded by an initial fascination in the 1950s, owing to the work of the pioneering British mathematician Alan Turing. Turing devised his eponymous 'Turing Test': that if a machine could trick a human into thinking it was human, then it had achieved human-level intelligence. (Few people would still agree with this conclusion, despite its influence.) Excitement turned to disappointment in the 1970s as artificial intelligence failed to deliver on its lofty promises. Interest rose again in the 1980s with the emergence of rules-based expert systems – algorithms for processing information – being applied extensively in commercial settings. This again proved a false dawn, with government research and development expenditure on AI and data science waning later in the decade.[3]

The wave of interest in data science that continued to gain ascendancy in the 2010s has emerged for rather distinctive reasons compared with previous waves. In this instance, excitement with data science has been driven by four novel factors. First, there is simply more data than ever before; with consumer devices, cameras, phones, sensors and more all constantly producing data. Second, the cost of data storage: both for disk storage, which is great for storing large volumes of data but poor for access; and for random access memory (RAM) storage, which is better for data access. Third, the cost of computer processing (doing things such as matching, counting, comparing or applying simple conditional rules to data) is lower than ever. And fourth, as we covered in Chapter 11, the advent of the cloud has allowed almost any organization to dabble in 'big data' and apply data science techniques, whereas previously they would have needed to acquire large, capital-intensive, costly, physical data infrastructure.[4]

In addition, high-profile applications of data science in fields as diverse as baseball, algorithmic financial trading and political elections have made data science more popular than ever. But critically, none of these reasons *per se* mean you should throw all your eggs in the data science basket. Data science – even with all the reductions in cost that have occurred – is expensive (a single, experienced, data scientist salary and associated hosting and analytics costs is likely to cost you a six-figure sum annually), and the return on the investment in certain sectors remains ambiguous. To have any hope of success, you first need to have a really clear sense of *why* you want to engage in data science techniques.

Putting the principle into action

Applying data science: the CRISP-DM approach

Set out in Figure 12.1, the cross-industry standard process for data mining (CRISP-DM) is an effective, open-source methodology used by data scientists and analysts. Its power comes in setting out a clear and easy-to-follow approach while reminding stakeholders interested in data science that data science *must serve a clear end goal.*

In the 'business understanding' phase, data scientists should work with stakeholders across the business – or a defined business unit – to clarify business objectives, understand the potential application of data science to these objectives, and develop a plan to test how data science could be used. For example, a large retailer that uses a membership scheme to provide discounts to members might be concerned it is losing members. The business objective might be to reduce membership churn and improve retention. It's incredibly important that at this point you set a *baseline level of performance* against which you can evaluate any future data science techniques. In other words, knowing 'how well do we currently make decisions on this issue?' and therefore being able to assess the difference afforded by future techniques.

In the 'data understanding' phase, work would involve investigating what data exists to address the membership retention issue. A data engineer or a data scientist would explore, test and check the quality of the data. The next phase of 'data preparation' would involve selecting, cleaning, interrogating and formatting data to render it ready for analysis – this is a huge part of a

FIGURE 12.1 The CRISP-DM cycle

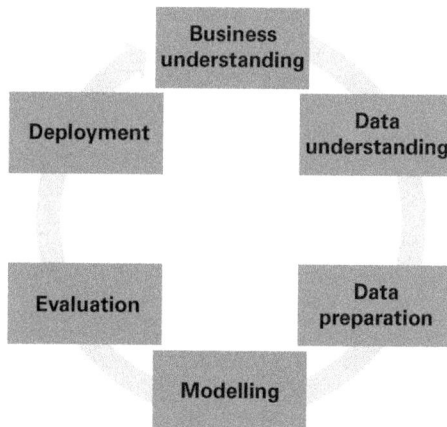

data scientist's job. Subsequently, the data scientist would move into the 'modelling' phase, choosing one or a variety of modelling techniques, and fit each of the chosen models to the data. This would all be aimed at understanding how membership churn could be reduced.

In the penultimate phase, the data scientist would then evaluate results. What has been learned? What should be modified? Do some techniques seem more effective than others? Further iteration might be made to the modelling approaches. All of this work has hitherto taken place outside of business workflows. In the 'deployment' phase, it's the job of the data scientist to take any techniques that have been proven effective through the evaluation phase and apply them to working practices. This might involve, for instance, providing new reports to teams focused on membership retention, encouraging them to try new forms of membership engagement. The impact of this work should continuously be reviewed even in the deployment phase, as user behaviours or external factors may lessen the effectiveness of the applied techniques over time.

As the CRISP-DM approach makes clear, the job of a data scientist isn't just fancy analytics. It covers data expertise, computer science knowledge, statistics and probability, understanding of business environments, communicating with stakeholders, data visualization skills, and understanding of data regulations and ethical considerations. Brilliant data scientists are thus, unsurprisingly, in high demand and there is limited supply. In Chapter 16 we cover means of recruiting or developing data science skills in your organization.

Problems that data science can address

A highly important skill of a digital transformation leader is to know when certain techniques can help solve real-life business problems. Much of this is learned through experience and trial and error. However, most successful applications of data science can be grouped into four types of analysis.

1. WHO OR WHAT IS THIS THING? (AND HOW SHOULD I THEREFORE TREAT THEM?)

If you are trying to change the behaviour of a user group – for additional sales, or a specific conversion goal, for instance – you first need to know who your users are. We have already covered in detail how user research (Chapter 7) can help in user identification. Now we can see how data science can supplement user research. Because such user identification is based on identifying patterns in datasets, it can also provide specific features of such user groups, which can be actionable by an organization.

This type of analysis is known as *clustering*. A data scientist would, based on available datasets, specify how many sub-groups or clusters they are looking for, and then run a clustering algorithm to segment and cluster data together to form different sub-groups. A very basic technique used for such *clustering* analysis is known as a *k-means* machine learning algorithm. The analyst would specify (and might iterate this based on results) a number of *k* clusters, and the algorithm would then group customers together based on certain attributes. Such attributes could include length of time they have been customers, geographic residence, various demographic data such as age or gender, revenue, site visits and so forth. A wide range of clustering techniques (most of which are more sophisticated than *k-means*) exist and a good data scientist would employ a variety of techniques and see which work best with different datasets.

An ecommerce company looking to optimize revenue through targeted online marketing campaigns might seek to use *clustering techniques* to group its customer base into various segments. An example segment might be: 'unmarried men over 45 years who live in suburban areas'. Once these segments are defined, the company could then trial different marketing approaches tailored to these segments, with the working hypothesis that personalized marketing would generate better returns than generic advertising. As always, while such data science insights can be hugely powerful, it requires business insight to sense-check whether the segmentation resulting from the analysis is meaningful.

2. HAS SOMETHING GONE WRONG?

Understanding if something is wrong – either by accident or intentionally, such as in fraud cases – is hugely important to enterprises. Data science can help through what is known as *anomaly detection*. The simplest approach involves creating rules – with the aid of someone who truly understands the business – and then applying these rules as a test against a dataset. For instance, a retailer might define the rule that 'no customer ever spends more than £1,500 on their first visit to a store'. This could be derived from just simple knowledge of the business. Thus, any time a transaction occurs that breaches this rule it could be held pending verification by someone within the business.

However, not all businesses – especially new ones – know enough about their operations to know what 'wrong' looks like. In instances like this, *clustering* analysis can be used to discover things that sit outside of segments – in other words, are *outliers*. Or, machine learning algorithms (which tend to be 'unsupervised' in so far as they have minimal human input compared with rules-based algorithms) can be trained – using *one-class classifiers* – to help to define datasets and thus understand what might constitute being an outlier. Where algorithms are trained, this requires data to be split into two: a *training set* to develop the model and a *test set* to then validate that the model works.

3. WHAT GOES WELL WITH THIS?

Winning new customers is hard. Therefore, being able to maximize value from existing customers is highly desirable for most businesses. This could involve cross-selling or upselling products or services. Data science techniques known as *affinity analysis* aims to group together things that are found together in datasets; in other words, they are *associated* with one another. This uses a statistical term known as *correlation*, which is where relationships between items are identified.

Such analyses – indeed all analyses – should be treated with caution as they may be a result of issues with data, or not the result of any causal relationship. As a consequence, a good data scientist should use statistical techniques such as 'support' – how frequently items appear together in a dataset – and 'confidence' – the probability that one occurrence of an item results in the occurrence of the linked item. These two terms will help to give a sense of likelihood whether the relationship is strong or not. When you see a pop-up next time you check out of a store online, or when you're asked if you'd like a particular drink with your order at a fast-food restaurant, you're probably experiencing the customer-facing end of *affinity analysis*.[5]

4. WHAT IF...?

Propensity modelling aims to predict how likely it is that a user will perform a certain action. This process involves using data on users over a defined period to determine the likelihood that a certain attribute – cancelling a subscription or making a purchase – will occur in the data. By using historic data, such modelling approaches are aiming to discover an algorithm that can be applied in real time to understand the current likelihood of user behaviour, and potentially devise new business actions to change the forecast scenario. For example, a targeted discount offer to a customer at a specific moment might reduce the likelihood of them cancelling their membership of a loyalty club.

Regression analyses are extremely versatile and can be applied in a wide variety of scenarios; they are particularly valuable in the machine learning field of data science. An asset trader, for instance, might wish to assess the valuation of a given item. Regression analyses could be used across a dataset to compare the relationship between different variables and how they might affect the price of the item.

In business settings, predictive models that can learn from new data and be continuously, and easily, updated are hugely powerful. If a travel agency wished to understand, for instance, 'what happens if we send this marketing to these types of customers?', a model that can be continuously updated and retrained on new sales information – depending on transaction volumes, something like a weekly basis may be appropriate – would be particularly valuable.

Exercising caution

It's easy to be wowed by data science. Unlike much of digital transformation, which we can easily see in our devices, the techniques and methods of data science lie hidden, 'under the bonnet' of digital activities. Not only does data science still have a relatively high bar to access in terms of learning how to use modelling tools like R, Python or SQL, it has its own language – both statistical and technical. If this chapter leaves you with only one lesson, let it be: don't be afraid to ask silly questions and apply common sense to anything that emerges from data science work. The stakes are too high to get data science applications wrong given how it is now used in everything from exam results to housing applications.

Below is a non-exhaustive list of 'silly questions' that you should use to exercise caution when presented with analytical findings:

• *What's our alternative means of making a decision?* Scepticism about data science techniques *does not mean refusing to engage or use data.* Quite the opposite. We should always seek to use data and analysis as part of any decision-making. But the point is whether we should rely on large data sets and advanced data science techniques *above other forms of analytical input*: user knowledge, basic data analysis, qualitative analysis and so forth. In other words, you need to evaluate the proposed new methodology against your baseline (ie previous or alternative) way of making the same decision.

- *What's the evidence that this is causation, and not mere correlation?* The statistics writer Tyler Vigen humorously demonstrated that high statistical correlations do not always imply causation in his book *Spurious Correlations*. In one of many examples, Tyler showed how the number of divorces in Maine had a 99.26 per cent correlation with the per capita consumption of margarine in the region. If you see a relationship suggested to you, interrogate whether it's plausible or not.[6]

- *What's the confidence interval around this?* This common statistical test can be applied in a variety of ways (it's more complicated if you have a non-normal distribution in your dataset – usually the case when extreme values occur) to give you assurance that a given figure, say the mean – average – of a dataset, lies within a range. A 95 per cent confidence interval means that you can be 95 per cent sure that a value lies within a stated range. The trade-offs between bias and variance are also important considerations when developing learning algorithms – you should ensure you understand the implications of these, and where and how trade-offs are being made.

- *Are we staying true to real life rather than getting swept up in the data?* Pause a bit here, because Bayes' theorem from the Tunbridge Wells born eponymous 18th-century statistician is one of the most powerful contributions to data science. It's best used when you know multiple probabilities: say the likelihood of a search term being a user searching for a specific film, and the general likelihood of a population searching for the film. It helps to account for false positives and can transform your understanding of probabilities. To take another example, the probability that an individual has cancer who has tested positive for cancer needs to take into account the wider probability of any randomly selected individual having cancer in the first instance.

- *Are the findings from our algorithms still valid?* Many algorithms – particularly machine-learning-based ones – are trained on historic data that captures human behaviour at a specific moment in time. But what if something changes user behaviour? Would the analyses still be valid? Many organizations found that algorithms developed based on user engagement before the Covid-19 global pandemic needed to be rerun, as user behaviour changed so significantly as a result of increased usage of digital devices that the algorithms were no longer valid. A whole suite of things could influence changes in user behaviour – regulations, economic recessions, marketing and so forth – and you should keep an eye out for what these may be and the impact they have on your algorithms.

- *Could our data be biased?* And what does this mean for our data science? This is part of a minefield of legal and ethical concerns that we will cover in more detail in Chapter 15. However, in short, data science is based on data, and data is captured for various reasons, almost never with the original intention for which the data science techniques are ultimately trying to apply. For example, much healthcare data is based on financial billing data capture, which, although it may provide analytical utility, is not optimized for patient care. Understanding who captures data, why, how and who may be excluded is hugely important to help you understand whether biases exist in the data that are exacerbated by any algorithm you develop. In addition, even if the data *per se* is not biased, it may reflect the realities of biased operating environments – humans making suboptimal decisions, for instance – and this needs to be factored into your considerations when applying data science techniques.

Where next?

As the CRISP-DM process sets out, first and foremost you need to use your digital roadmap and identified user needs as the starting point for any data science considerations. Depending on the expertise within your team, you may feel it necessary to reach out to either internal or external data science experts to run a workshop covering the first parts of the CRISP-DM cycle. An individual with particular expertise in data engineering should be the first type of specialist to turn to, as they will give you a sense of what is possible from your datasets. Once you've analysed a few potential areas of investigation for data science application, you can move to a short, sharp, iterative pilot exercise. The discovery approach set out in Chapter 9 can guide you. Here you'll be testing whether it's worth exploring further and thus investing more in data science resources. Don't be afraid to pull the plug early. There are real, potentially transformative gains from data science, but it's an expensive business and you need to work out what your risk versus return appetite is before committing too much too soon.

BRINGING THE PRINCIPLE TO LIFE
The successes, failures and yet still huge potential of data science

Data science hit the consciousness of many business executives in a big way in the early 2010s with a story uncovered by the writer Charles Duhigg. Outlined in the *New York Times*, Duhigg chronicled how the US retailer Target, through analysing customer sales, was able to 'identify about 25 products that, when analysed together ...[could]... assign each shopper a "pregnancy prediction" score. [Target] could also estimate her due date to within a small window, so Target could send coupons timed to very specific stages of her pregnancy.' Such was the precision of Target's analytics that its methods hit the headlines when an irate father complained to the company that his teenage daughter was being inappropriately targeted with pregnancy coupons, when, unbeknownst to him and his daughter, she was indeed pregnant.[7]

Yet for each Target story there are tales of disillusionment. We learned earlier in Chapter 7 that nine in ten executives felt that their artificial intelligence investments had failed to deliver any financial benefits.[8] Relevant for many critics of big data and its potentially negative impact on citizen privacy consideration, a White House panel concluded that the US National Security Agency's extensive collection of citizen phone records and calls, and presumably subsequent use of data science techniques to mine such data for insights to prevent terror attacks, could not find 'a single instance in which analysis of the NSA's bulk metadata collection actually stopped an imminent attack, or otherwise aided the Government in achieving any objective that was time-sensitive in nature'.[9]

The trends that have underpinned the explosion of interest in data science this time around aren't going away. Despite the setback and disappointments, there are many use cases of data science being applied effectively across all sectors now. As the Target and NSA stories demonstrate, the challenge now going forward will be twofold: to continue to find instances where data science can offer true value to consumers and businesses and maximize the benefits from these instances; and to build trust among users, wider society and regulators that this data is being used safely and appropriately.

Tips and tricks

- So much of data science comes down to using statistics and probabilities well. It's probably been a while since you did maths at school, so really don't be afraid to reacquaint yourself with some of the basics.

- Data science uses a range of software technologies and applications. Get yourself familiarized with some quick introductory online courses. You can do all the reading you want, but there's no substitute for getting your hands dirty.

- Reach out to data science experts early. Someone with a good knowledge of data environments and different analytical techniques will be able to judge relatively quickly if more investigation is warranted. Simply insufficient or inaccessible data are common and easily identifiable reasons for why your data science aspirations may never become a reality.

- Always be sceptical until you see real-world impact. All the modelling and fancy visualizations in the world cannot trump actually demonstrating how data science practically benefits your organization and customers.

- Be inquisitive about the data and use a customer's mindset. Where does the data come from? What data does your organization hold? How would a customer feel if they knew what you know about them? Apply a simple sense-check about how someone outside of the company might feel about their data being used this way.

What you might say in your next meeting

We're going to dip our toe into the waters here, but let's retain a healthy scepticism throughout.

Don't expect immediate benefits. We need to go through a proper process and evaluate whether this is working for us.

Up to 80 per cent of a data scientist's job is to prepare the data for analysis. This isn't cheap. So that's why it's so important we record and store data in a format that is consistent and potentially valuable for data science.

Let's do a statistics primer with the board before we do the full data science presentation.

What's the confidence interval on that?

Where you can find out more

John D. Kelleher and Brendan Tierney's *Data Science* (MIT Press, 2018) is a brilliant and practical guide to the subject matter and an inspiration for some of the practical guidance in this chapter. David Stephenson's *Big Data*

Demystified (Pearson, 2018) does exactly as promised and is an important reminder of the infrastructure requirements associated with data science. David Spiegelhalther's *The Art of Statistics* (Pelican, 2019) is a must-read for any business executive or public sector leader, regardless of interest in data science. And, for those fascinated by the history and potential future of data science and AI, check out Michael Wooldridge's *The Road to Conscious Machines* (Pelican, 2020). *The Batch* weekly newsletter from deeplearning.ai is also a great resource to keep abreast of developments.

Notes

1 Kelleher, JD and Tierney, B (2018) *Data Science*, MIT Press, Cambridge, MA

2 Wooldridge, M (2020) *The Road of Conscious Machines: The story of AI*, Pelican, London

3 UK House of Lords report on Artificial Intelligence (2018) *AI in the UK: Ready, willing and able*, 16 April. publications.parliament.uk/pa/ld201719/ldselect/ldai/100/100.pdf (archived at https://perma.cc/7HCM-UYRN)

4 Stephenson, D (2018) *Big Data Demystified: How to use big data, data science and AI to make better business decisions and gain competitive advantage*, Pearson, Harlow

5 This is covered in great detail in Kelleher, JD and Tierney, B (2018) *Data Science*, MIT Press, Cambridge, MA

6 Vigen, T (2015) *Spurious Correlations*, Hachette Books, London

7 Duhigg, C (2012) How companies learn your secrets, *New York Times*, 16 February, www.nytimes.com/2012/02/19/magazine/shopping-habits.html (archived at https://perma.cc/C6Y2-D8UN)

8 Ransbotham, S, *et al* (2020) *Expanding AI's Impact with Organizational Learning*, Boston Consulting Group, 20 October, www.bcg.com/publications/2020/is-your-company-embracing-full-potential-of-artificial-intelligence (archived at https://perma.cc/BN7W-9AJD)

9 Liptak, A (2013) Judge upholds NSA's bulk collection of data on calls, *New York Times*, 27 December, www.nytimes.com/2013/12/28/us/nsa-phone-surveillance-is-lawful-federal-judge-rules.html (archived at https://perma.cc/PB7U-EKBN)

13

Stimulating innovation

Whether a start-up or an established enterprise, successful innovation is hard – but possible.

The principle in a nutshell

While the term 'innovation' conjures up images of eccentric scientists and fantastic ideas, it's important never to lose sight of the end goal of innovation. No company should seek to be innovative for the pure sake of innovation. Innovation needs to serve a business purpose. Ultimately, it needs to add value to an organization, an ecosystem or customers, in ways that break free from established approaches.

Doing the same thing faster or cheaper isn't innovation. Doing something different is. It's best to think of innovation as one of two things: either doing existing things differently, or doing entirely new things. If both add substantially more value to your organization and customers than what you were doing before, consider that innovation. Sometimes innovation can be what was termed by the late management thinker Clayton Christensen as 'disruptive innovation' – this is where an innovation entirely upends a market and its market leaders, creating *new* types of markets and demand; think AirBnb and established hotel chains, for instance.[1] But it doesn't always have to be disruptive to be worth doing. Any innovation that improves on the status quo significantly is valuable.

What's the problem being addressed?

Innovation is notoriously difficult. Different-sized and -shaped enterprises struggle with it in different ways:

- *At big companies, innovation is typically stifled by bureaucracy,* hierarchies and established ways of doing things. A long-standing business of any value will have honed and developed processes for delivering value to its customers. The most obvious thing to do is to seek to make those processes leaner and efficient, rather than entirely change them. This efficiency pressure often makes a hostile environment for innovative ideas.

- *At small companies and start-ups, the challenge is often how to innovate frugally,* on a low budget. While necessity can often be the mother of invention, as the saying goes, it can also just make innovation hard. Trying to build the next driverless car company on a shoestring budget isn't very plausible.

- *For all types of organizations,* doing a bad idea for too long can be problematic. Killing an idea that's going nowhere is often harder than it seems for emotional, political and financial reasons. Pursuing a dud project can cast a long shadow across many innovation efforts.

These aren't easy problems to fix, but a proven approach to generating innovative ideas and solutions can address all of them: the double-diamond process.

Putting the principle into action

Popularized by the British Design Council, the double-diamond methodology builds on the work of the systems thinker Béla H. Bánáthy and his book *Designing Social Systems in a Changing World* (Springer, 1996). Bánáthy articulated that in design thinking – a creative approach that puts users at the heart of all problem-solving – innovation is best achieved through a two-step process. This begins with *divergent thinking*, where many potential ideas and solutions are generated, and then progresses to *convergent thinking*, where the best idea is whittled down, refined and developed.

Figure 13.1 demonstrates an adapted version of the double-diamond approach. It covers four phases, which, though can be iterative and link back to one another, should be broadly followed sequentially. The approach is best undertaken by a multidisciplinary team; thoughts, ideas and

FIGURE 13.1   The double-diamond methodology

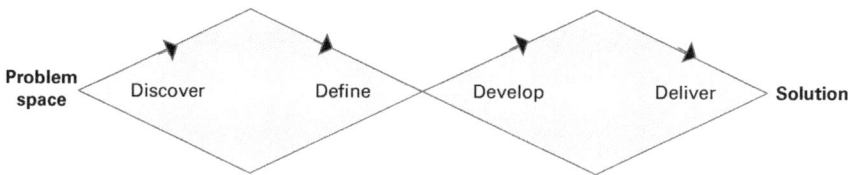

approaches from different disciplines in your organization must all be welcomed. Innovation comes from new ways of thinking about and seeing the world. Asking the same transformation team in the same organization to 'just be innovative' isn't going to work.

However, innovation cannot be simply mandated by boardroom decree. Many organizations find that while a culture of continuous experimentation and curiosity can be fostered across employees, albeit with considerable time and effort, the core of innovative thinking and doing is often best guarded by a small group of innovators. At NASA, despite having 10 field centres and over 17,000 staff, the space agency focuses its innovation efforts at the Ames Research Centre in Silicon Valley. This is where 'the character of rebels' is represented, according to its former director Dr Pete Worden, and hosts the innovative thinkers in the organization.[2]

The double-diamond process starts not with a predefined problem, but with a 'problem space'. This is because – from the perspective of innovative thinking – having a well-defined problem may result in a well-known solution. If you ask the question, 'how do we improve sales of E-Z learning online software by 23 per cent by next year?', you're likely to get an answer about marketing and pricing. If you instead start at the problem space, 'how do we offer more value to our customers?', you open the door to much more lateral thinking. Such thinking is behind many 'moonshot' concepts, as described by the economist and political scientist Mariana Mazzucato.[3] The point about these big, huge, complex problems – such as global warming or reducing inequalities, for instance – is that they are not easily reducible to simple problematization. They have multiple dimensions, sometimes conflicting. And they are ripe for big thinking, which innovation handsomely lends itself to.

In the discover phase, you should spend time doing user-centred analysis, much like that set out in Chapter 7. This way, by talking to real people, you'll get a better sense of what actually matters to them. You might also find value in doing exercises like *surveys*, *user personas* and *journey mapping* to identify pain points for users. In the define phase, by broadening out your thinking, you can now start to converge on a more precise definition of the problem. In our earlier E-Z learning online software example, your user research might actually lead you to conclude that the problem is, 'while we have points of differentiation, our customers don't have a clear sense why they would choose our products over our competitors.' Once you have this definition, you should start generating and refining ideas for solving the problem. You might use techniques such as:

- *Brainstorming:* create a safe space for individuals to suggest ideas without judgement.

- *Analysis:* using data to understand which issues matter more than others to users.

- *Secondary research:* which could be desk-based research, interviews with experts, or exploring purported 'best-practice' case studies (though always take these with a pinch of salt – you might find it's worth thinking about: who's writing the case study, why are they writing it, how can they evidence improvements, and were these improvements sustained?).

- *Prioritization:* using established criteria (such as benefit or impact and cost or effort) to move some of your long-listed potential solutions to short-listed ones.

By the end of the first diamond, you should have a small number (perhaps even just one) of ideas that you want to take forward for development in the design phase. Here you should start to *prototype* a solution (much like we covered in Chapter 9). This can take all forms: drawn prototypes, physical prototypes, mocked-up screens, actually coded software or simplified hardware and devices. The point is you want to be able to get a sense of what the solution might look like in reality.

In the deliver phase, it's all about evaluating your prototyped potential solution(s). You can do this with user testing, analysis of potential benefits, and by following overall evaluation criteria. These might be more granular that in the define phase, and cover areas such as:

- *Strategic fit* – if we took this idea forward, would it fit with what our organization is trying to do strategically?

- *Potential for positive impact* – could this idea bring significant improvements to people beyond what they currently have (some organizations use a '10x' factor consideration)?

- *Feasibility* – how realistic is it that we could actually achieve this?

At the end of the deliver phase *it's incredibly important that you are not afraid to kill ideas, even good ones*. At Google's X innovation lab, the typical ratio of ideas that get past this stage is less than 1 in 100.[4] There is no shame in this. In fact, many at X see it as a sign of healthy innovative development that so many ideas are discarded.

Where next?

If you do take an idea forward at the end of the double-diamond process, this is where you need to start building it in earnest and incorporating it in how your business works. There are a few potential avenues here:

- *piloting* the new innovation in more areas and evaluating it further, before rolling out across the whole organization;
- *implementing immediately* across the organization;
- *keeping it separate* from the organization, and creating a separate business unit.

It would be desirable to categorically state that one approach is better than another, but the reality is more complex. The piloting approach is certainly wise in most instances, as it affords the possibility of ironing out unknown bugs or issues before wider rollout. The immediate implementation approach is usually high risk, but potentially high reward if you're in a race against competitors to bring a new innovation to market. And the separate business unit idea comes with many academic supporters – notably Clayton Christensen – who highlight how hard it is for established businesses to adopt new innovations.[5] In many instances, these businesses' established ways of working and cost structures create barriers to adoption of innovation. But not all organizations have the luxury of running 'innovation units' and so this may not be practical for your company. If this is the case, it's important to set realistic metrics by which to judge the success of the innovation; if it really is a new way of doing things better or a new thing to do, don't use your old corporate KPIs by which to judge it. Seek to judge it on its own merit instead.

BRINGING THE PRINCIPLE TO LIFE
Lessons in moonshots from Alphabet's X

So what does good innovation look like in practice? Well, you may not have the resources of Alphabet – the parent company of Google – but there are still some great lessons to be learned from the successes of X, also known as the 'Moonshot Factory'.[6] Its list of successful innovations – and failures – makes for fascinating reading: Waymo, the driverless car company valued at $105 billion in 2020; Brain, which created the widely used TensorFlow open-source machine learning neural network tool; and of course, Google Glass, the eyewear which became a cultural phenomenon in the early 2010s but was subsequently shut down.

Indeed, though only a few of X's projects 'graduate' into the Alphabet corporate mainstream, often these 'graduates' are still shut down: Loon, which aimed to create an internet network available to all across the world via flying balloons in the stratosphere, was made a subsidiary of Alphabet in 2018 but subsequently wound up in 2021. The lesson of not being afraid to kill ideas, even promising ones, is a good one. Doing otherwise risks falling victim to the *sunk cost fallacy* in economics, whereby good money is thrown after bad just because it's believed to be too hard to stop.

Another important lesson from X is the way its teams focus on the hardest problem first. This is known as the 'Monkey First' tenet. The thinking goes that if your problem was how to get a monkey to recite Shakespeare while standing on a pedestal, don't start with the easy problem of building the pedestal. Instead, go straight to the (at the risk of understatement) hard problem of teaching a monkey to recite Shakespeare. This way you should quickly find out if the whole endeavour is pointless or not, because the hardest problem is impossible – or at least is *currently* – to solve.

X also, as per the double-diamond thinking, has a roaming 'Rapid Evaluation' team. It's their job to critically appraise ideas quickly, beginning with a 'pre-mortem' whereby the teams are asked to imagine a world where it's all gone wrong. By starting with the possible failures, potential blockers to future development can be identified and either addressed, or the initiative be wound down.

In your organization, you may not have the multi-billion-dollar budget X has, but you can start small, prototype, evaluate and focus on the hardest problems first.

Tips and tricks

- Being innovative means making things radically better. Think big: 'how can we make this at least 10 times better than currently?'

- There are many parallels to be found between the double-diamond process and the service design process. The key difference with the former is that when you're looking to innovate, it's not just about meeting user needs; it's about making something that is *significantly better than* and *significantly different from* the status quo.

- Avoid setting success criteria that you'll never meet, like overly ambitious financial targets. This will kill innovative ideas early.
- Start with the hardest problem first. The rest should then follow.
- Set a timeframe and some goals from the outset. Be prepared to retire the idea if you fail to meet the goals. And if you do, celebrate the learning rather than criticize the failure.

What you might say in your next meeting

If we're serious about innovation, we need to think big – what are the huge, intractable issues we face?

Do we really know the true problem we're trying to solve yet?

Who's going to pay for this innovation? If we do it, we need to give it time and space to fail.

Let's celebrate failure. This is partly a numbers game. We won't get it right the first, tenth or maybe even one hundredth time.

It's OK for innovation not to be for us right now. We need to prioritize efforts as an organization.

Where you can find out more

Some great articles on moonshots, X and innovation are cited in this chapter, which are worth reading. However, for a different kind of medium, try listening to the technologist Azeem Azhar's interview with the CEO of X, Astro Teller, on Azhar's podcast *Exponential View*.[7] For more on the double-diamond approach, check out the British Design Council's website at www.designcouncil.org.uk

Notes

1 Christensen, C, *et al* (1995) Disruptive technologies: Catching the wave, *Harvard Business Review*, January–February

2 De Jong, M, *et al* (2015) The eight essentials of innovation, *McKinsey Quarterly*, 1 April, www.mckinsey.com/business-functions/strategy-and-corporate-finance/our-insights/the-eight-essentials-of-innovation (archived at https://perma.cc/WPD7-WHUP)

3 Mazzucato, M (2020) *Mission Economy: A moonshot guide to capitalism*, Penguin, London

4 Franklin-Walls, O (2020) Inside X, Google's top secret moonshot factory, *Wired*, 17 February, www.wired.co.uk/article/ten-years-of-google-x (archived at https://perma.cc/72VC-GKY9); Ghosh, J (2021) Lessons from the moonshot for fixing global problems, *Nature*, 19 January, www.nature.com/articles/d41586-021-00076-1 (archived at https://perma.cc/7WGH-6G2R)

5 Christensen, C (1997) *The Innovator's Dilemma: When new technologies cause great firms to fail*, Harvard Business Review Press, Cambridge, MA

6 Franklin-Walls, O (2020) Inside X, Google's top secret moonshot factory, *Wired*, 17 February, www.wired.co.uk/article/ten-years-of-google-x (archived at https://perma.cc/U3XA-73SQ)

7 Harvard Business Review (2020) Inside Alphabet's X: Nurturing radical creativity [Podcast], Season 4, Episode 22, hbr.org/podcast/2020/04/inside-alphabets-x-nurturing-radical-creativity (archived at https://perma.cc/NA3X-WN5F)

PART FOUR

Future-proofing

Learning and innovation go hand in hand. The arrogance of success is to think that what you did yesterday will be sufficient for tomorrow.

WILLAM POLLARD

The American physicist William Pollard's quote points to a painful truth in digital transformation: you can never rest on your laurels. Your customers are unlikely to continuously thank you for something you did years ago. In short, you will only ever be as good as your next success. In this part, we cover how to ensure you are prepared to meet this ongoing demand.

In Chapter 14, we address the hugely concerning rise of cyber crime and what you need to do to protect your organization now and in the future. In Chapter 15, the thorny issue of ethics is addressed. Technology may be ideologically neutral, but how it is applied is anything but. Being an ethical organization won't happen by happy coincidence – you will need to work at it. In Chapter 16, we look at how to bring in the skills and talent needed to make digital changes a reality. And in Chapter 17, we review a few trends that are likely to affect the digital world over the next 20 years.

In the Conclusion, 10 principles are set out that affirm what we've covered in this book and that should guide you through your digital efforts. In the Appendix, we use a simplified example of a health and care ecosystem to try, one final time, to demystify some of the stubbornly confusing terms and acronyms that regularly crop up in the lexicon of digital transformation.

14

Protecting and defending your organization

Make your organization cyber-secure by design.

The principle in a nutshell

Cyber crime is a real and serious threat to any organization. Money, reputation, fraud and the functioning of your business could all be lost in a cyber attack. Estimates suggest that in 2025, cyber crime will cost the global economy some $10.5 trillion – more than the entire value of the illegal drugs trade combined.[1]

Unfortunately, the same trends that make data science possible (Chapter 12), coupled with the increasing sophistication of cyber criminals and a poorly concerted global response to cyber crime, means that cybersecurity is unlikely to drop down the boardroom agenda any time soon. While we still maintain a strong focus on traditional measures of security in business (who would leave their office permanently unlocked?), we're playing catch-up in confronting the challenges posed by cybersecurity. Indeed, in the United Kingdom, for several years now, you're more likely to be the victim of a cyber crime than physical violence or robbery.[2]

As a digital leader, your job is to understand the nature of threats posed to your organization, develop a plan to contend with the threats and deliver on the plan. Remember that this will need to be an iterative process; like everything in the world of digital, data and technology, new issues emerge quickly. You need to stay abreast of developments and be prepared to react accordingly.

What's the problem being addressed?

Cybersecurity covers a whole world of considerations. Broadly speaking, cybersecurity means putting in place measures to prevent the theft, damage or disclosure of information, data or services from your organization through protecting the networks, systems and devices of your organization. Given the variety of threats and potential avenues of attack, you need to take an end-to-end view of the problem. The UK National Cyber Security Centre provides a helpful framework for doing so.[3] It recommends:

- *Understanding the risks your organization is exposed to:* depending on the nature of your organization, its data assets and its underpinning technologies, your risk exposure profile will vary.

- *Implementing appropriate mitigations:* it's important to tailor mitigations towards your risks. Cybersecurity can be expensive and investing significant amounts in areas of negligible risk would be unwise.

- *Preparing for incidents:* even the best protected organizations can suffer potentially devastating cyber attacks. You need to be ready to react when incidents occur so you can minimize damage.

While many cyber attacks have technical names, it's important to remember they are ultimately caused by humans (or at the very least, initiated by humans). And your organization's biggest cybersecurity weaknesses will most likely be the result of human error – weak passwords, individuals being conned into giving out sensitive information, coding errors and so forth. So don't be blinded by the technology – maintain a common-sense approach throughout as you plan, prepare and implement your cybersecurity approach.

Putting the principle into action

Understanding types of threat

With so many potential avenues of attack – known in the cyber language as 'vulnerabilities' – it can be hard to know how to prioritize defence efforts. Figure 14.1 shows, on a scale of 1 to 5, the top 12 cybersecurity concerns from over 1,200 IT security executives in a global survey by the market intelligence company Statista as of late 2020.[4] It's important to understand each in turn, so that you can plan your defence accordingly.

FIGURE 14.1   Top cyber security concerns, 2021

Cyberthreats by level of concern, 2021

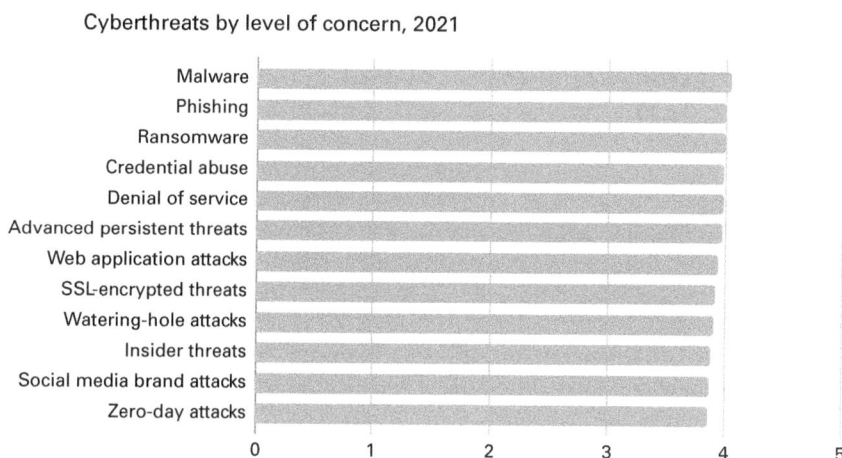

Malware: a type of software deliberately constructed to cause damage to a computer system. Types of malware vary. Worms can self-propagate and infect other computer systems and users as soon as they have breached a system; they can easily spread across networks and cause huge damage. Viruses act similarly; however, they need a trigger, activated by a computer user (usually unwittingly) before they can spread. Spyware is developed to gain access to information about you, which is then relayed back to external users, usually with the intent of creating harm (although much is often shared back to advertisers too). Trojans can be similarly toxic. They enter systems by masquerading as benign applications, hence the name.

Phishing: whereby fake messages – usually via email, text message or sometimes phone – are sent to a user, purporting to be genuine (an insurance or tax payment request, for instance) but actually intent on extracting sensitive information from a user. Often credit card details are the target for phishing attempts. 'Spear phishing' is a form of phishing whereby there is an intended target user, such as a chief executive.

Ransomware: a form of malware. Once inside a computer system the software will typically use encryption – which is usually a means of translating and protecting information from misuse by converting plain text to an unreadable format, known as 'cipher text' – to lock a user outside of their system, and then demand a ransom payment to let the user back in. The UK National Health Service was subjected to a WannaCry ransomware attack in 2017, affecting up to 70,000 devices.

Credential abuse: is where stolen credentials – usually a username and password – are used to enter a computer system undetected. From here the hacker may try to extract information, change operations and generally cause issues of potentially huge damage. Credentials can be accessed either by phishing, or processes known as credential stuffing – where automated processes try out a high volume of potential passwords on known logins in order to access an account – or sheer brute force of attempts (a process which may also be semi-automated).

(Distributed) Denial of service (DDoS): where a flood of messages, connection requests or other forms of internet traffic are targeted to a specific part of an organization's technology stack – usually a network resource such as a server or website – which overruns the capacity of the resource, thereby causing the service to cease to function. This is usually temporary, though could cause permanent damage. Attacks are most effective when using multiple computers as part of the assault. DDoS attacks are analogous to sending fleets of vehicles to deliberately jam up a motorway.

Advanced persistent threats (APTs): often non-state actors or terrorist groups will try to – undetected – access a computer system and remain there for as long as possible, gathering information and intelligence to be used against the host entity. What differentiates APTs is usually a motivation that is beyond financial, most likely to covertly gather insights and knowledge on a target over a sustained period of time.

Web application attacks: as we covered in Chapter 8, thanks to the internet, web applications have provided an amazingly powerful way to simply and effectively interface between users and web servers and database servers. This connection is both a strength and potential weakness. Most web applications cannot make use of firewalls or secure sockets layers (SSLs) because websites must be made open to the whole public. This, coupled with the fact that web applications often need a direct access connection to databases which potentially store sensitive customer data, makes them particularly vulnerable to attack.

SSL-encrypted threats: SSL certificates are usually a sign that a website is protected and safe to use for things like financial transactions. However, hackers may seek to dupe users by obtaining cheap or free SSL certificates to give the appearance of safe sites. Such sites are often linked to phishing emails. An SSL site can be identified by a padlock icon on a web browser.

Watering-hole attacks: here, hackers target well-used websites by an intended victim. The hackers penetrate the website and place malware on the site, with the intention that the malware infects the intended victim. Given that these websites are likely to be trusted by the intended victim, often a remote access Trojan (RAT) may be downloaded (unintentionally) by the victim that allows hackers to have back-door access to their systems. 'Drive by attacks' – where malicious code is inserted unbeknownst to the user – are also possible.

Insider threats: as described, this is where an either intentionally malicious or simply negligent actor sabotages or steals valuable and confidential information from within an organization.

Social media brand attacks: where a company experiences sustained attacks across one or more social media platforms where the reputation of the company is vilified, usually with highly shareable and consistently repeated content that denigrates the company.

Zero-day attacks: is the descriptor given to the window of time when a vulnerability is simply unknown to the host organization. In the absence of knowledge, this leaves enormous potential for damage and the only way this can be mitigated is either by becoming aware of the vulnerability, or by inadvertently fixing it, for instance by a patch or software upgrade.

The list above isn't comprehensive, though it's a good start. Other issues to worry about include:

- *Man in the middle attacks:* also known as 'eavesdropping attacks' – where a malicious entity manages to listen in on a conversation between two people who think they are just talking to each other, gaining confidential information in the process.

- *Botnets:* these are a means of delivering cyber attacks. Computer networks, often vast in scale, are used to run botnets for attack purposes such as phishing, brute force or DDoS attacks.

- *Exploit kits:* rather like a code repository such as GitHub (covered in Chapter 9), exploit kits are repositories of malicious software made available to hackers to launch automated threats with minimal effort.

- *Code or SQL injections:* many websites require data to be passed from an external user to a site, such as inputting a customer account number. If poorly constructed, a hacker can inject malicious code into the website, which could then be passed to the web server, which is in turn made vulnerable to the hacker.

- *Social engineering:* remember that humans are the weakest link in your cybersecurity chain. Social engineering attacks involve compromising and pressurizing individuals – through blackmail or threats, for instance – to hand over sensitive information.

Putting your defences in place

Feeling a little bit terrified? You should be. There are a lot of bad actors out there aiming to cause harm. It's almost implausible that you won't be an intended victim of a cyber attack, either personally or corporately, in the next working year: just check your spam folder in your emails for evidence. Below are the most common types of defence you should be employing to protect you.

Database, network and infrastructure security: your network and infrastructure will cover routers, firewalls, servers, storage systems, intrusion detection systems (IDS) and domain name systems (DNS). Each of these are vulnerable to attack. The US Cybersecurity and Infrastructure Security Agency (CISA) lists a number of wise defences, including: physically and virtually separating elements of the network to best protect sensitive information; operating a principle of 'least privilege' so that users are only given access to the minimum, as opposed to the maximum, information they need; implementing good wireless security, such as strengthened passwords; and using firewalls (which can automatically filter out dangerous traffic).[5] If you have physical servers on premises, these must be securely guarded and protected. Ensure all database software management is up to date with any upgrades to protect from any known vulnerabilities.

Data security: first and foremost, you need to understand what data you have, where it lies and who has access to it. Your data security approach should involve using techniques to avoid unauthorized access, using encryption to scramble data, and carefully protecting encryption keys to allow access to data. Use of virtual private networks (VPNs) can also help secure and encrypt data access once data is being used by users.

Identity management: users present a very high-risk point of failure for an organization. Just like you need to understand where your data sits, you need to understand who has access to your organization's software and hardware. Once you have this information, you must very clearly keep a log of access controls and ensure that only authorized users can access your systems and network. Again, the principle of 'least privilege' should guide your access permissions.

Endpoint user and device security: many users in your organization – particularly with the rise of remote working exacerbated by the Covid-19 pandemic of the early 2020s – will use a variety of devices (mobiles, laptops, personal computers, etc) to access your organization's network. Ensure that these devices are only in the right hands and that each device is secured with strong passwords and two-factor authentication (such as entering a password and code received to a separate device).

Application security: ensure applications are up to date with patches and upgrades so that most recently discovered vulnerabilities are covered and afforded protection.

Disaster recovery and business continuity planning: in the event of a catastrophe or disaster, ensure you have a clear plan to recover information and ensure your business operations can continue as far as possible. This may include separate backups of data, alternative devices, separate network connections and putting in place contingency workflows that can operate under different cybersecurity attack scenarios.

Standards and certification: international standards are available to guide best-practice cybersecurity. These vary from industry and geography, although the family of standards known as ISO/IEC 27000 are a good starting point. To gain certification, your organization must put in place and clearly demonstrate compliance against the standards, which is then externally verified by a certifier.

Getting the basics in place

So what are some core basics you need to do? First, make sure your organizational *leadership is committed to cybersecurity*. Chief information security officers (CISOs) or similar are becoming increasingly common in companies with the sole responsibility of cybersecurity across an enterprise. However, you don't need a CISO to show leadership. Ensure someone on your board – and ideally an executive *and* non-executive board member – is responsible for overall cybersecurity. In some territories, such as Europe and the UK, GDPR regulations require this by law.

Second, solidify your *networking security by running a series of penetration tests*. This is where a paid actor, acting on your behalf, tries a series of ways of attacking your network and identifies vulnerabilities which you can then mitigate. Third, ensure *applications are up to date with the latest upgrades for cybersecurity*. Web applications, as discussed, are particularly vulnerable, and make sure you understand where the points of risk lie with them. Fourth, *implement staff training*. This should involve everything from secure password management to understanding what to do in a disaster recovery scenario.

And finally, implement *strong password management*. Anecdotally – accurate data is hard to come by as many organizations are reluctant to share how often they have been attacked – poor password management is one of the most common methods of attack for cyber criminals. Ensure all staff use secure passwords with two-factor authentication.

Where next?

Make sure you have a named cybersecurity lead in your organization. This may end up being you. You should then – either internally, or by procuring a cyber expert organization – do a review of your vulnerabilities. This should address your risks, mitigations and then prepare plans to put in place if the worst happens. Importantly, you need to constantly horizon-scan the cyber-security landscape. Your cyber plans should be iterated and updated as new risks emerge.

Documentation is critical. Make a secure list of key users, devices, databases, network components and applications and forensically ensure they are as protected as possible. This audit trail will also be essential if you plan to achieve cybersecurity accreditation. Such certificates are usually part of a wider service from an accreditation provider. Such providers can be helpful for both the advice they bring and the training they may offer employees in your organization.

BRINGING THE PRINCIPLE TO LIFE
Cyber attacks and the unintended consequences of social media

It's not hard to find horror stories of cybersecurity attacks. Ransomware, malware, network hacks and the like can be found from everything from the aviation sector to marriage infidelity sites. These are serious and hugely costly, financially speaking, breaches. However, in this case study, a slightly different but nonetheless potentially enormously damaging type of attack is covered: social media attacks.

In 2019, the US JP Morgan subsidiary Chase Bank ran a Twitter campaign about #MondayMotivation telling consumers to cut back on expenditure such as coffee, taxis and going out to eat. The full tweet read:

> You: why is my balance so low/Bank account: make coffee at home/Bank account: eat the food that's already in the fridge/Bank account: you don't need a cab, it's only three blocks/You: I guess we'll never know/Bank account: seriously?

Politicians, consumers and even the celebrity Paris Hilton jumped onto the Chase Bank tweet hashtag and vociferously criticized the bank for 'poor shaming'. Here was a deliberate attempt by an organization to run a campaign which violently backfired; thousands of negative tweets were launched against the company, significantly harming its reputation in the process.[6]

In this instance, Chase Bank had failed to plan ahead and 'pre-mortem' what could have gone wrong with its campaign. However, additional work could have been done to track social media sentiment. Most platforms now allow applications, via APIs, to provide social listening services to provide alerts back to the company when negative comments occur in high volumes. So remember, you can put in place great cybersecurity protection, but you still need to dynamically scan your organization for new and emerging risks and threats – some of which can even be self-inflicted.

Tips and tricks

- Think like a hacker. What do you have that is valuable to them? How can you therefore best protect it?
- Plan for as many scenarios as possible, and make sure your plans have a wide variety of permutations within them. Don't get too precise. You don't need to worry about exactly how much a ransomware attack might demand financially. You do need to worry about what to do if a ransomware attack happens.

- Your registry of users, applications, network and infrastructure, and devices is itself incredibly sensitive. Protect it closely.

- Keep your wits about you if under attack. Cybersecurity is about reacting to a threat effectively as much as planning for it.

- Reach out to external support. At least at the start of your cybersecurity planning, you won't know what you don't know – external expertise can help inform you.

What you might say in your next meeting

What's our cybersecurity strategy?

Who's responsible for cybersecurity here?

If someone makes a ransomware attack on us and demands payment, what do we do?

Do we need cybersecurity accreditation?

Are all our employees trained and aware of our cybersecurity risks? How do we measure compliance?

Where you can find out more

The UK National Cyber Security Centre provides excellent guidance and resources for individuals and organizations of all sizes. Many other countries have comparable organizations. Depending on where you're based, familiarize yourself with these organizations. Dip into the resources. And consider taking up some of their training.

Notes

1 Morgan, S (2020) Cyber crime to cost the world $10.5 trillion annually by 2025, *CyberCrime Magazine*, 13 November, cybersecurityventures.com/hackerpocalypse-cybercrime-report-2016/ (archived at https://perma.cc/KZ9L-AQ4H)

2 Ashford, W (2019) Crime stats show switch in focus by cyber criminals, *Computer Weekly*, 24 January, www.computerweekly.com/news/252456397/Crime-stats-show-switch-in-focus-by-cyber-criminals (archived at https://perma.cc/5DVZ-SG4M)

3 UK National Cyber Security Centre (2020) *10 Steps to Cyber Security*, www. ncsc.gov.uk/files/2021-10-steps-to-cyber-security-infographic.pdf (archived at https://perma.cc/QGG8-B9HZ)

4 Statista (2021) Most concerning types of cyberthreats according to IT security decision-makers worldwide as of November 2020, April, www.statista.com/ statistics/500946/worldwide-leading-it-security-threats/ (archived at https:// perma.cc/BG5L-ZNVN)

5 Cybersecurity and Infrastructure Security Agency (2018) *Securing Network Infrastructure Devices*, 21 June, us-cert.cisa.gov/ncas/tips/ST18-001 (archived at https://perma.cc/R9PF-SLWR)

6 Greenspan, R (2019) Not everyone was so motivated by Chase's Monday Motivation, *Time Magazine*, 30 April, time.com/5580255/chase-bank-monday-motivation-tweets/ (archived at https://perma.cc/L575-A5PQ)

15

The ethical digital organization

Being an ethical and responsible organization doesn't happen by magic – you need to work for it.

The principle in a nutshell

Being ethical is no longer a 'nice to have' for an organization. While business scholars have been at pains to point out that ethical organizations – here defined as diverse, unbiased and progressive – are likely to perform better than peers in terms of profitability, this focus on classic considerations of shareholder maximization rather seems to miss the point.[1] Though there may be a business case for 'doing the right thing', this rather calculating approach to ethics risks undermining the very endeavour because it may seem inauthentic to the people most affected: customers and staff.

In the eyes of many customers, the businesses they buy goods and services from reflect something about themselves; if your values don't align, you're unlikely to be chosen by such customers. And, in the simplest way possible, few people like to think of themselves as 'bad people'. Digital staff are in high demand and tend to be of a relatively young age profile – millennial or Gen Z – for whom values and purpose are extremely high in considerations when choosing an employer.[2] Unethical organizations will find it hard to attract the best talent. However, remember: doing the right thing should not be seen as a choice, it should be an expectation.

What's the problem being addressed?

So what constitutes being an ethical digital organization? It's probably one for the philosophers to debate – and indeed, firms like OpenAI, DeepMind,

Facebook, Microsoft and Google have all hired philosophers to advise on ethics within their artificial intelligence teams – and certainly will change over time. But five questions should provide a good starting point for your ethical considerations:

- Have we removed biases from how we work?
- Do we place our customer privacy at the heart of our operations?
- Is our workforce diverse and reflective of the society we wish to see?
- Are we committed to sustainability?
- Are the products and services we make accessible and inclusive?

The answers to each of these points will vary between organizations, but first we need to start by engaging with the questions.

FIGURE 15.1   A framework for being an ethical organization

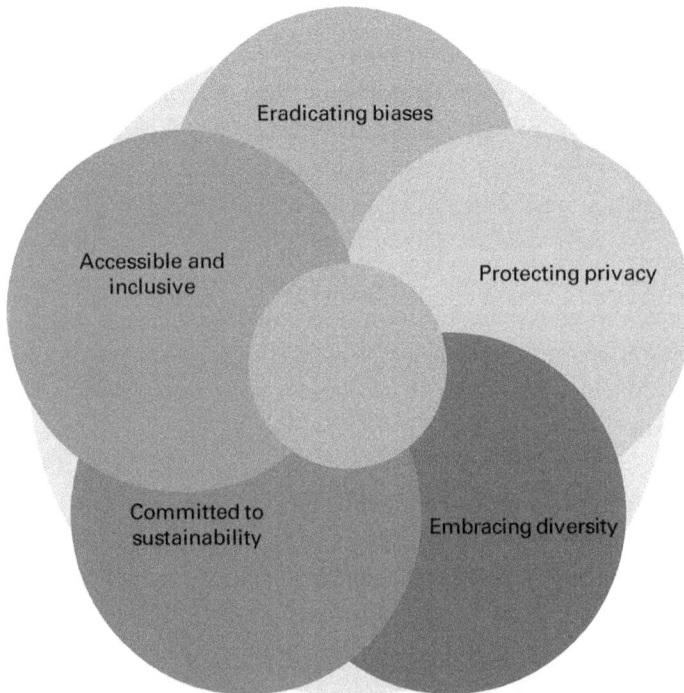

Putting the principle into action

Conscious and unconscious bias

Conscious bias should – in theory – be easy to eradicate. It is effectively the deliberate discrimination of individuals or groups in society. An organization that proactively gives a lesser training offer to, say, pregnant employees because it fears a lower return on investment in case the individuals do not return from maternity leave would be engaging in conscious bias. This should never be done and would most likely be illegal in any jurisdiction. You should be intimately aware of the law around these issues. In the UK, the Equality and Human Rights Commission sets out the protected characteristics which no organization should ever discriminate against.

There are some times where conscious bias may be possible, or at least commercially defensible. For instance, a hotel chain seeking to entice new customers might run digital marketing campaigns that proactively target married couples in the belief that these are its target demographic. This is a form of conscious bias, but probably within the realms of being acceptable. This example should highlight the thorny and complex area of bias. As an organization, you may wish to commission external experts to advise you and your workforce on such issues so you can get a better handle on what is or is not acceptable.

Unconscious bias is by turn even harder to spot. This is where deep societal issues exogenous to your organization may be subtly causing biases in your company, unbeknownst to you. Social norms or networks, such as public schools or universities, are frequently pointed out as potential sources of unconscious bias, particularly in recruitment. Individuals may be tempted to recruit 'who they know' or 'people like me' rather than the best qualified and equipped individuals for a job, which may perpetuate barriers to entry to organizations as a result of social hierarchies and inequalities.

Data science and artificial intelligence has also been identified as a realm prone to unintentional bias. For instance, the use of predictive policing across law enforcement agencies has been highly controversial. Using historic data and algorithms to predict potential crime hot spots, the 'PredPol' approach has been criticized for perpetuating biases in racial profiling in policing. Effectively, if the data is based on biased practices, the data will most likely perpetuate biased practices.[3]

So what can you do about this? Starting with a clear understanding of the key activities of your organization should be the first port of call. This will cover everything from internal things like paying people, hiring people and so forth, and external things such as the products and services you make and sell. Go through each one and try to identify potential areas for bias. Using protected characteristics as a rule-of-thumb for groups which may be particularly affected can help. It's also incredibly important to include key parts of your supply chain in this analysis. While you may be free from bias, if a key supplier of yours is guilty of gender-based pay discrimination, for instance, how can you plausibly claim to be an unbiased organization in the eyes of your customers?

Encoding privacy

Data privacy is likely to define this current age of digital transformation. How organizations and governments use personal data has become a frequent concern of business leaders and policymakers. Such concerns have increased in intensity since the sensational WikiLeaks revelations by the former US National Security Agency contractor Edward Snowden in 2013. Subsequent revelations of how political campaigns used personal information in the 2016 UK Brexit referendum and US presidential campaign of Donald Trump have only heightened sensibilities.

Since 2018, countries in the European Union and the UK have been bound by the General Data Protection Regulation. This provides clear principles, measures, safeguards and punishments for ensuring data privacy is upheld in organizations. The most important underlying principle in GDPR is the regulation's first statement: '[that] the data subject has given consent to the processing of his or her personal data'. From this devastatingly simple principle much follows. Organizations must seek consent, record it and demonstrate it.

Despite the hugely positive strides that GDPR has made in improving protections for individuals with regards to their data rights, grey areas remain as to when consent is given, or fully required. Few individuals truly understand what they are consenting to when agreeing to enable 'cookies' when accessing a website. In a nutshell a cookie is a tag downloaded onto your computer which identifies you to a website. It records the sites you have visited, what you have clicked on, and how long you have looked at particular pages. Such cookies are invaluable to digital advertisers and help to explain many of the pop-up adverts you undoubtedly experience. Yet though individuals have given *consent*, through learning how an organization is actually using their data, disappointment, anger and indeed confidence in the organization may be eroded. As you think through your privacy approaches, obviously at a bare minimum you must comply with all legal regulations. However, you should go beyond this and be user-centred in your thinking: how would your customers feel if they knew how you were actually using their data? If this is in any way likely to evoke negative emotions, what should you do about it? Writing – in plain language – how user data is utilized and how individuals can exercise choice in the use of their data would be a wise move.

Ensuring a diverse workforce

The technology industry is particularly afflicted by a lack of diversity. The problem became a widespread public issue in the early 2010s in the US, leading to annual diversity reports from the Silicon Valley technology giants being published. However, despite increased attention, little has improved. In 2020 in the UK, only 5 per cent of leadership positions in the technology industry are taken up by women and only 4 per cent of the entire technology workforce come from a black and minority ethnic background, compared with a national black and minority ethic population of nearly 14 per cent.[4]

The root causes of the lack of diversity in the technology sector are complex and challenging for any single organization to overcome. Many of the issues stem from societal pressures, education and skills pathways, and a lack of familial role-modelling. However, there is still much that organizations can – and should – do to help improve diversity. The experiences of one firm – 2020 Delivery, a UK-based public services consultancy – highlights some of the options available to companies. In the first instance, 2020 Delivery recognized it had a problem in that it lacked diversity, particularly at leadership levels of the organization – a common issue in professional services firms. The company sought external expertise from a diversity and inclusion consultancy to undertake an audit of its practices, recommend solutions and to provide staff wide training in diversity and inclusion. Four concrete changes arose that many organizations seeking to improve diversity should embrace.

First, specific targets were set – at board and wider corporate level – for improving workforce diversity within set timeframes. These were signed off by shareholders and progress against these targets was reported at board level. Second, new recruitment processes were established with the help of the Applied recruitment platform, which ensures recruitment is unbiased. Names of applicants, their backgrounds and any educational institutions were removed from the recruitment process, for instance. Third, new pathways for potential applicants were developed, with concerted efforts focused on outreach campaigns at institutions that did not traditionally provide routes into professional service advisory firms. And fourth, new parental leave and allowances policies were implemented, to help bridge and overcome any potential gender gaps. All of these approaches are considered best practice for improving diversity in the workforce and should be considered by any firm as part of its digital recruitment efforts (covered in more detail in Chapter 16).

A path to sustainability

In terms of wider societal issues, you don't get much bigger than tackling the climate crisis. All organizations will need to demonstrate the role they can positively play in this battle. This will require adhering to regulations and laws that will undoubtedly emerge during the course of the 2020s. Decarbonization and achieving net zero emissions will be a critical requirement.

Much like with diversity, digitally progressive organizations should understand their own emissions currently and set targets for becoming carbon neutral. Many governments have set 2030 as a goal, and this should be considered a good starting point. Progress against such targets needs to be tracked on a regular interval and reported at board level.

In terms of digital transformation, you should be aware that many digital practices are surprisingly carbon-intensive. Data servers, cloud computing, blockchain and computer processing in general – everything from emails to Zoom meetings – all carry a carbon footprint. Researchers found that training a natural language processing algorithm could emit over 200,000 kg of carbon dioxide – more than quintuple the emissions of an average car, including the processes involved in the car's manufacture.[5]

Important techniques to cover in your decarbonization plans should include: reducing travel, particularly air travel; minimizing office estates and footprint; reviewing entire supply chains and switching to low emissions suppliers – particularly regarding logistics; and, where appropriate, using carbon offsetting techniques.

Accessible and inclusive services

If you work in public services, it's likely the services you make will need to be universal – that is, accessible by all. This means ensuring that your services – in the UK, this is by law – need to be inclusive and not discriminate against any group. For example, this will mean writing copy in plain English (and other languages where appropriate), applying colour-blindness tests, making sure that if they are web services, they work on all browsers, can operate in areas of low internet bandwidth and so forth. You may also need to provide additional services to ensure that people with certain impairments – such as visual impairments – can access services. You may even provide physical kiosks or call centres that individuals can contact if they need help.

If you work in private sector services, there is a slightly more nuanced consideration when it comes to accessibility. In some instances, you may wish to proactively 'design out' certain customer groups. An ecommerce store probably doesn't want to spend too much effort developing services for people with low or no digital literacy or confidence. However, you should be careful about proactively excluding too many customer groups – in short, you don't know what you might be missing out on. Some start-ups, for example, only design smartphone applications for the Apple iOS operating system in the belief – well founded – that iOS customers tend to be more wealthy. Yet while that may be true on average, there are far more Android users than there are iOS users. By being exclusive, in other words, you may end up missing out on many great customers.

Where next?

Your board should already have ethical issues at the top of its mind. If it doesn't, you might need to write a paper so it can quickly get on top of the issues. Being ethical is the job of everyone in the organization, but it also must be led from the top. Use the framework in Figure 15.1 and related questions to form a diagnostic of how your organization currently performs. From here, you should aim to have an open discussion among senior leaders in the organization about where you need to be, and what the action plan should be to get there. As stated at the start of the chapter, you should not seek to be ethical because the 'business case stacks up' – you should be ethical because it's the right thing to do. And be sure, you will fall behind the competition if you're not: customers are coming to expect sustainable, ethical and progressive values to underpin all organizations. If you fall behind these expectations, expect to be punished.

BRINGING THE PRINCIPLE TO LIFE
How everyday data discriminates against half the population, with deadly consequences

Data is neutral and unbiased, right? Sadly, this is a pervasive and hugely misleading myth. As the writer and activist Caroline Criado-Perez has brilliantly demonstrated, many technological developments have been based on data derived from the experiences and expectations of men – to the detriment, at times fatal, of women.

In one of the most jarring of the accounts in Criado-Perez's award-winning 2019 book *Invisible Women: Exposing data bias in a world designed for men*, Criado-Perez shockingly exposes how women are 47 per cent more likely to be seriously injured in a car crash than men.[6] The reason? The crash-test dummies used by car manufacturers in safety tests are designed overwhelmingly with men in mind. For decades, the only dummies used were based around a '50th percentile' (in terms of height and weight) concept of a man. It was only in the 2010s that any form of female crash-test dummies was used, and these were hardly representative. Not only were they not actually designed to anatomically represent women, but they were also only tested in passenger seats. Worse still, no tests were done for pregnant women, despite the fact that car crashes are a leading cause of foetal deaths.

Many tests and regulatory requirements for vehicle manufacturers, producing reams of data, may have given a false sense of safety and objectivity. Though much data was available, the underlying data was biased – designed by men largely with men in mind. Disturbingly – yet often the case – there are legal provisions in place that should prevent such injustices. As Criado-Perez notes, Article 8 of the Treaty of the Functioning of the European Union states that, 'in all its activities, the Union shall aim to eliminate inequalities, and to promote equality, between men and women.' Unfortunately, this is a stark reminder that just because the law mandates something and just because you have data doesn't mean that the right thing is being done. It's your job as a digital leader to have this in your mind throughout if you wish to lead a truly ethical organization.

Tips and tricks

- Think like your customers: what do they expect from you? If you're falling short, what will you do about it?
- Do an audit of your workforce using protected characteristics as a guide. Are you reflective of the society in which you operate?
- What are the points of decision-making in your business that are most susceptible to biased thinking? What data or information is used to inform decision-making and how do you ensure bias doesn't creep in?
- Be transparent. If you're on a journey towards sustainability, don't be afraid to say. Customers would rather know you're acknowledging a problem and tackling it than hear nothing at all. By saying nothing, you risk giving the impression you don't care.
- Make sure you know of all the laws and regulations that affect your digital transformation. If necessary, get legal advice to ensure you're compliant. Some of the fines can be extremely hefty for failing to comply.

What you might say in your next meeting

Are we compliant with all GDPR requirements? How do we evidence this?

What's our target for being net zero?

How do we help our staff contribute to our decarbonization efforts? Do they know what we need them to do?

What's our approach for removing unconscious bias in our organization?

We have great values – do we know if all our suppliers share our values?

Where you can find out more

Caroline Criado-Perez's aforementioned *Invisible Women* (Vintage, 2019) is a must-read for its range of examples and eye-opening evidence of how data can blind us to biases. Any wise digital leader should read up on the EU's GDPR regulations. Even if you don't operate in jurisdictions that must comply with GDPR, it's still considered leading practice. In the US, there is no federal equivalent, although individual states have their own regulations you need to stay abreast of.

Notes

1 Georgescu, P (2017) Doing the right things is just profitable, *Forbes*, 26 July, www.forbes.com/sites/petergeorgescu/2017/07/26/doing-the-right-thing-is-just-profitable/?sh=2bf927ef7488 (archived at https://perma.cc/C8W9-TS3X)

2 Pelisson, A, *et al* (2017) The average age of employees at all top tech companies, *Business Insider*, 11 September, www.businessinsider.com/median-tech-employee-age-chart-2017-8?r=US&IR=T (archived at https://perma.cc/F4KF-BJW5)

3 Baldridge, J (2015) Machine learning and human bias: an uneasy pair, *TechCrunch*, 2 August, techcrunch.com/2015/08/02/machine-learning-and-human-bias-an-uneasy-pair/ (archived at https://perma.cc/U9NC-A6Q2)

4 Yahaya, G (2020) The UK tech industry has a race problem – if we don't close the gap we will fall behind, *Evening Standard*, 3 September, www.standard.co.uk/comment/comment/the-uk-tech-industry-has-a-diversity-problem-if-we-don-t-close-the-gap-we-will-fall-behind-a4539391.html (archived at https://perma.cc/Y36L-TRZB)

5 Strubell, E, *et al* (2019) Energy and policy consideration from deep learning in NLP, *Proceedings of the 57th Annual Meeting of the Association for Computational Linguistics*, July, www.aclweb.org/anthology/P19-1355/ (archived at https://perma.cc/7ZDS-FMRE)

6 Criado-Perez, C (2019) *Invisible Women: Exposing data bias in a world designed for men*, Vintage, London

16

Upskilling and bringing in new talent

The success of your digital transformation depends on the talent you have access to.

The principle in a nutshell

You cannot become a digital organization without talented and skilled digital experts. Even if you go down the route of strategically outsourcing many digital capabilities, you still need experts in your organization to procure and manage these outsourced capabilities.

Upskilling digital capabilities doesn't happen by magic either. You need to identify high-potential individuals, give them the time and space to build up their new capabilities and provide them with the experiences – either within your own organization or outside it – to develop their skills.

Digital talent is in high demand. You won't just be competing on salaries. Such is the scarcity of technology specialists that you'll also need to be a great employer, flexible and most likely one that fits with the values of your employees. In a world of high demand and low supply, it's the digital specialists who can have their pick of the best jobs.

What's the problem being addressed?

Talent management and development is hard in any context. Getting it right requires aligning your strategy with your budget constraints and operating environment. Often even the smallest changes can have huge unintended consequences. Bringing on board a new digital specialist to a generalist organization may mean breaking established pay scales. How do you explain this to other staff? What development trajectory do you put these new specialists on? Who is ultimately responsible for quality-assuring their work, and so forth?

There are four broad options when it comes to developing digital skills:

- developing talent in-house;
- recruiting permanent staff;
- recruiting temporary staff;
- forming strategic partnerships with third parties.

Each has their pros and cons and needs to be carefully evaluated. It's quite possible that you may end up with a hybrid model, as well as one that changes over time as your needs evolve.

Putting the principle into action

Split by job family, Table 16.1 details the *key digital and technology specialist roles* you may need to recruit at differing points in your digital transformation. You almost certainly won't need all of them, and those that you do need may not be full-time roles. Nevertheless, it's important to get a full grasp of the potential roles out there.

TABLE 16.1 Key digital and technology roles

Job family	Role	Responsibilities
Leading and managing	Product manager	Overall leadership of digital teams. Interfaces with senior executives. Prioritizes team efforts and sets strategic direction for teams.
	Delivery manager/ Scrum master	Enables digital teams to focus on their core responsibilities. Takes bureaucracy and hassle away from team members. Leads agile ceremonies and working practices. If working with software engineering teams, should have skills in DevOps delivery techniques.

(continued)

TABLE 16.1 (Continued)

Job family	Role	Responsibilities
Understanding users	User researcher	Responsible for being the voice of the users in the digital teams. Expert in user research techniques and practices. Can communicate the importance of user-centred design approaches to senior stakeholders.
	Service designer	Uses techniques such as service or journey mapping to document, analyse and improve upon user experiences and journeys. Understands the importance of design in improving digital experiences.
	Content designer	Expert in using language (also sometimes known as 'copy') and visuals to communicate with users. Content designers play a key role in the look and feel of digital products and services.
Using data effectively	Business analyst	Can blend deep understanding of business requirements with user needs, thus guiding the thinking of digital teams. Able to pinpoint which issues are most important through using quantitative and qualitative techniques. Some potential overlap with data science skills in terms of simple analyses (usually adept at historic or simple predictive analyses).
	Data scientist	Can spot and capitalize on opportunities for using data science techniques to improve business processes and meet user needs. Should be well versed in basic data science approaches. Able to train and maintain algorithms and communicate their outputs and conclusions to stakeholders. Data scientists should be well aware of ethical concerns around data science, and place a high premium on protecting and abiding by data protection laws and privacy regulations.
	Data engineer	Specializes in managing and maintaining databases and datasets. Ensures the data is structured appropriately and that data quality and integrity is of requisite standard. Should understand data science techniques and be able to identify what data engineering is required for machine learning algorithms to be developed.

(continued)

TABLE 16.1 (Continued)

Job family	Role	Responsibilities
Developing and building	Technical architect	A critical role that is able to review existing technology stacks, advise on future ones, and can set the overall vision for how developer teams can build, maintain and run services and products. May have broad knowledge across all domains – known as 'full stack architects' – or be specialized in a few key stacks.
	Front-end developer	Also known as 'client-side developer', these are responsible for creating and maintaining the software aspects that users most clearly see. Needs to be expert in technologies such as HTML, CSS, DOM and JavaScript. If creating mobile applications, most likely will need expertise in development environments that are non-web based, such as React Native, which allows iOS and Android development. If a client-side developer has capabilities and experience on the server side, they may also be known as a 'full stack' software engineer.
	Back-end developer	Also known as 'server-side developer', back-end developers can integrate the work of front-end developers to allow applications to be hosted and run on databases. Back-end developers need to be expert in programming languages that allow such integrations like Ruby, Java, Python, PHP. Should have good familiarity of working with APIs across a range of platforms. If a server-side developer has capabilities and experience on the client side, they may also be known as a 'full stack' software engineer.
	DevOps engineer	A DevOps engineer sets up the infrastructure used by the front- and back-end developers. In a cloud environment, infrastructure can itself be set up by lines of code, so the DevOps engineer is responsible for writing the software which sets up environments for development, testing and live. The engineer should ensure that the environments behave identically and will scale up and down with demand.
Securing and protecting	Cybersecurity analyst/engineer	Responsible for overall cybersecurity planning and implementation. Can either conduct or manage teams to run a variety of key tests such as penetration tests and vulnerability scanning.

(continued)

TABLE 16.1 (Continued)

Job family	Role	Responsibilities
Promoting and marketing	Digital marketing	A constantly changing field, but given the importance of ecommerce to any digital organization, a vital skill set. Digital marketers should be able to implement and oversee and deliver a range of techniques and skills: search engine optimization; keeping abreast of search algorithm changes; managing marketing campaigns on major platforms such as Google and Facebook.
Buying digital	Procurement specialist	Digital procurement specialists should be able to help you source, buy and contract-manage digital suppliers. They should know key frameworks to use, be able to advise on benchmark pricing, and know how to exit contracts or transition suppliers with minimal disruption.
Managing digital	Service operations lead	Covers a wide variety of roles to ensure upkeep of services and may manage a team or suppliers who provide this service. May be well versed in service management techniques such as those of the Information Technology Infrastructure Library (ITIL). Where hardware is involved, this could include providing help desk support to clients when issues occur. For both hardware and software, this role should be able to plan for improvements, outages and disaster recovery incidents.

Strategic options for bringing talent into your organization

It's certainly possible to *develop the skills* involved in all of the roles listed in Table 16.1. It's largely a function of time and experience. If you're keen to try and retrain staff to be able to fulfil these roles, you need to ensure you can actually give them the necessary experiences to really learn these skills. You may need to be creative here. If you are at the start of your digital transformation journey, are staff realistically going to have the opportunities to learn the skills you need them to? If not, consider secondments to friendly organizations. Alternatively, you may consider sponsoring or part-sponsoring some qualifications or courses for them to take. One-year master's degrees in data science are becoming increasingly popular with employers, whereby staff take a year off – fully or part-funded – to learn data science skills which they can then come back to their host organization and implement. Many online courses exist – from HBX, Coursera, Udacity, CodeAcademy and DataCamp, to name a few – which can allow staff to build new digital skills on a more part-time basis. If you wish to go down this route, it's vital you give staff the time to actually undertake this learning (these are usually very involved and time-consuming courses) and, most importantly, opportunities to test their newfound skills in anger in the workplace.

Recruiting new digital skills is of course a tried and tested approach. Here you have two options: permanent or freelance. In many instances, particularly when recruiting skills in the 'developing and building' job family, jobs are in such high demand that many individuals prefer to stay freelance due to the high day rates they can command. If you are truly wedded to the prospect of recruiting staff permanently to these roles, you need to consider at least two factors: first, can you actually justify the costs (experienced developers and data scientists in the early 2020s can easily command over £100,000 per annum in salary costs); and second, are the people you are recruiting for aligned to your technology stack? While most skilled specialists can retrain to new program languages, this is often suboptimal, especially if you are paying high prices. With this in mind, it may make sense to go for a hybrid mix of some permanent and some freelance staff.

An alternative approach is to form *strategic partnerships* with suppliers that can provide you with specific digital capabilities; these are usually developer capabilities, but could be any capability listed in Table 16.1. While this may have many attractions in terms of cost and flexibility, be careful when signing any contracts – ideally you will want to be protective of all intellectual property developed by teams working for you, regardless of whether they are from a third party or not.

If you are reliant on third parties for many of your digital capabilities yet do have the budget to recruit some specialists in-house, it's sensible to recruit internal roles that make you an *intelligent client* of suppliers. This means hiring roles that have the technical knowledge to assess, manage and oversee digital suppliers effectively; usually this would mean bringing product manager, technical architect and business analyst roles in-house.

In all instances, you should have a view as to whether your digital specialists need to be *on-shore* or *off-shore* (meaning staff being situated in your company's main country of operations or outside of it, respectively). The remote working practices of the early 2020s brought on by Covid-19 have demonstrated to many employers that there is little real trade-off with off-shore working, and there may be many financial benefits to be gained;

typically off-shore digital specialists are less costly than on-shore. However, you need to give due thought as to how this might affect team dynamics; where your data is stored (for some organizations there remain requirements for data to be processed in specific jurisdictions); time differences between team members, and firewalls and restrictions between countries (which is particularly the case if working with these or staff based in China).

Evaluating digital skills when you have few digital skills

A huge challenge facing any organization looking to quickly ramp up its digital skills is 'how do I know what good looks like?' If the hiring organization has little internal expertise, it risks facing a real information asymmetry: how can you tell if a developer's code is any good if you can't code yourself? Fortunately, a variety of differing approaches can help.

First, reflect on whether there are obvious qualifications or certifications for the roles you are hiring for. You might require, for example, that a data scientist has a qualification in a field such as computer science, physics, maths or engineering. However, it's important to note that many digital specialist roles don't have obvious alignment to traditional academic qualifications and remember that *having the qualifications is no guarantee that you can do the role in a business environment*. Second, when recruiting, you should – where appropriate – ask to see examples of things that your potential employees have worked on before. Ideally, these would be products that you could use to seek to understand the role the individual played in developing them. Many developers will share examples of code they have written – usually via a repository such as GitHub – with prospective employers, so they can be reviewed. If you don't know what you're looking for here, you may wish to employ a few days of a software engineer to review the code and give you feedback with their thoughts.

Third, it's still OK to use competency-based interviews with candidates, asking questions like: 'give me an example where you solved a problem such as X.' While you may not be able to interrogate all of the technical aspects of the candidate's approach, it's vital to remember that your digital specialists will form team environments, and such interviews are helpful in assessing team working and collaboration skills. Fourth, set general exercises for candidates. Imagine – or use actual – professional scenarios such as 'we have two potential technology stack options – how would you help us assess which one is best?' Analysing the approach candidates take will help you get an understanding of their logical thought processes, which is ultimately what underpins any technology job.

And fifth, it's a good idea to use panels composed of internal digital experts and, where necessary, external digital experts. The latter you may need to remunerate on a per diem or per hour basis. These panels can sit in on the interviews or review exercises. A variety of experiences and knowledge on such panels can help ensure you get a rounded view of candidates.

Where next?

Once you have your digital roadmap, you should start fleshing out what skills you are going to need and when. When you have a clear sense of this, compare it with the resources you have currently. The gap will help to guide your recruitment efforts. It's quite possible the gap will be so large that this affects your roadmap – effectively you may need to push back and delay certain initiatives due to a lack of resources. This may well be wise and reflects the necessarily iterative nature of digital transformation. While you could throw money at the problem and try and hire more digital staff, faster, you need to make sure you have enough capacity to oversee the work of these digital teams effectively too.

BRINGING THE PRINCIPLE TO LIFE
Scaling up digital capabilities quickly in an advisory firm

When The PSC, a public service specialist consultancy (formerly known as 2020 Delivery, which we came across in Chapter 15), sought to build its digital capabilities, it had relatively few digital specialists in-house. As such, it adopted a hybrid and multiple-pronged approach to developing digital skills.

First and foremost, The PSC's leadership made it a strategic priority to build a healthy, profitable and well-regarded digital business within a year. It developed a roadmap of internal and external digital projects. The nature of these projects shaped the company's resourcing requirements for the year. Second, the company made the strategic decision to run a hybrid resourcing model; a few digital specialists would be hired permanently and these would manage a small number of external digital specialists, hired on a fixed-term contractor basis. The permanent digital specialists were recruited using an expert digital recruitment agency dedicated to improving diversity and inclusion in the technology sector. Importantly, the recruitment agency was also run by experts who themselves were technologists, meaning they helped to bridge any gaps in The PSC's technical awareness with regards to recruiting.

Third, The PSC created an apprenticeship model development programme to upskill staff in digital ways of working. This was a competitive programme which staff had to bid to join. The staff were then dedicated to digital work on a quarterly rotating basis and given additional digital training and development from a suite of online course providers. This focused time and the internal digital roadmap work meant the individuals were given the necessary time and experience to build their digital capabilities.

The result was that in under a year, the company was able to go from one digital specialist in the company to ten, with ten further experts available near-shored on a contractor basis. This resourcing allowed the company to win major digital projects for leading organizations such as the UK Space Agency and NHSx – the National Health Service's innovation and artificial intelligence agency.

Tips and tricks

- Use your digital roadmap as your starting point. Use this to guide what digital resources you need.

- Set a budget. If you're likely to go over, reprofile your roadmap to fit the budget, rather than try and cut corners.

- Don't try and do everything in-house from the start. As you build out your capabilities, you'll learn more about what you need in-house and what can be contracted out.

- Avoid outsourcing all technology expertise. Even if it's just procurement capabilities which you retain in-house, at the very least you need people who know what they're buying and whether it's working or not.

- Remember where ultimate accountability lies. If you're bringing on board digital resources that you don't understand, how can you be truly accountable for them? Either upskill your own knowledge, or make sure accountability lies with someone who does understand.

What you might say in your next meeting

People are going to make our digital transformation happen, not machines.

If we hire in haste, we risk repenting at leisure.

To evaluate something, you first need to understand it. We need some digital capability on our evaluation panel.

Let's accept we need help here – there's no shame in working with a specialist digital recruitment agency, even if HR's noses are put out of joint a bit.

On-shore or off-shore – is that really our biggest worry?

Where you can find out more

Digital recruitment is actually one of the hardest places to find honest, independent advice. A lot of money is there to be made, and is made, from organizations placing or brokering digital talent in organizations. As such, the internet is full of sites telling you this or that, but in reality, you need to keep your wits about you and remember it's in their interest to make money from you. Nevertheless, it's recommended to reach out and speak to a few digital recruiters to get a sense of what they can offer you and whether you like them. Be prepared to pay around 20–25 per cent of first-year salary to the recruiter for each recruit.

17

Defining the next horizon

You always need to be looking ahead in order to stay ahead.

The principle in a nutshell

Digitally advanced organizations never stand still. They are constantly on the lookout for new opportunities. Though they focus on optimizing operations in the here and now, they are not afraid to rip up the rulebook and embrace new technologies if they present a possibility of making significant gains on competitors.

Keeping your eyes on the next horizon isn't the same as adopting or buying a new technology every time you read or hear about the latest fad. Doing that is likely to waste a lot of money and disappoint many. The history of technology is littered with so-called 'game-changing' innovations that failed to change anything. Your job is to keep an inquisitive yet sceptical eye on future developments. You need to set ground rules for how and when your organization invests in potential future technologies. In short, are you a lead innovator or a follower? Either can work, so long as it aligns to your overall objectives.

What's the problem being addressed?

How can you tell a technology dud from one that revolutionizes society? Why did Facebook succeed where Friendster and Myspace, relatively speaking, failed? The answer is a combination of people, products and pure chance. You can't legislate for all of these and nor should you try. Sometimes things that seemed like failures were just ahead of their time. Barcodes were invented in the early 1950s, yet it wasn't until the 1970s that they began to revolutionize inventory management and indeed was only in the 2020s when barcode's underlying technology – adapted to become QR codes – took centre stage in many efforts designed to battle against Covid-19.

Broadly speaking, we are in the third age of internet technologies. The first, in the 1990s, gave rise to the internet, and with it a previously unimaginable level of human connectivity made most visible in the rise of emails, instant messaging chat, web portals and directories of information. The second phase, from the 2000s to the 2020s, saw the emergence of cloud computing, high-speed broadband connections, social media networks, ecommerce, mobile devices and platform-style marketplaces.

The big question for your digital transformation is thus: what does the next era hold? Figure 17.1 sets out a framework for thinking about how changes in the future might arise. Importantly, note the prominence of the bucket of 'chance': an unforeseen (if not unforeseeable) ecological, political, humanitarian or cultural incident or movement can change much received wisdom and established practices. You need to be agile and nimble in reacting to such potential changes. In the following section we explore some of the likely trends that you should factor into your thinking when developing future digital roadmaps. Be warned – predicting the future is a fool's errand (though, of course, this is precisely what data scientists aim to do), so please treat the following pronouncements with due caution.

FIGURE 17.1   A framework for horizon scanning

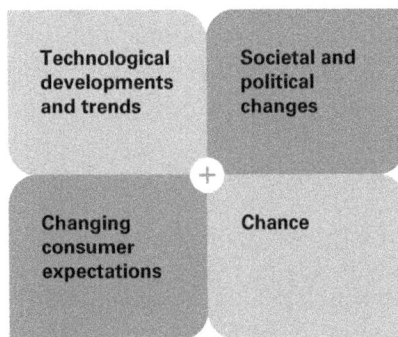

Putting the principle into action

With the necessary caveats in mind, below are some critical trends to be aware of that may make a big impact on digital transformation work over the next 10 to 20 years.

The 'platformization' of everything – by a few giants...

According to the market intelligence firm Statista, during 2020, Google was responsible for nearly 9 out of 10 internet searches. StatsCounter's estimates during the same timeframe put Facebook's share of social media activity at nearly 70 per cent. The market research firm Canalys put the combined share of the cloud computing market of the three main providers in 2021 – Amazon Web Services, Microsoft Azure and Google Cloud – at over 58 per cent.[1] These figures highlight the extent to which a few major technology giants effectively control the digital world. More pertinently, and unsurprisingly, these giants are intent on continuing to do so. The 'everything-as-a-service' model discussed in Chapter 11 is highly attractive to these firms – effectively, the model would help them capture as much internet activity as they possibly can. So expect your developer teams to continue to need to integrate with the APIs of these beasts, and as they make changes to their operations be aware of major knock-on implications for your operations (if Facebook stopped integrations with certain critical applications in your technology stack, for instance). You will need to stay nimble and abreast of the developments of these major players.

...yet expect a backlash led by decentralized movements

The client–server relationship that dominates the current digital age hugely enriches the large technology players that dominate the server side. So every photo you post on Instagram or tweet you dispatch on Twitter is captured as data by these respective companies. This data is then used to improve the companies' operations or target advertising at you. The rise of blockchain and decentralized technologies is an attempt to disrupt the client–server dynamic. Instead of relying on a few large server providers, decentralized, distributed networks are formed across individuals' computer systems. Cryptocurrencies and non-fungible tokens are based on such underlying technology.[2] It's likely that certain institutions and companies will embrace this new approach. Ultimately, it gives the promise of lower transaction costs by removing third-party margins and potentially greater security. In your organization, you should keep an eye on the technologies developed under decentralized models and continuously judge whether they afford you the necessary benefits to justify adopting them.

Regulations will tighten on the digital economy

The advent of GDPR regulations marked the start of what is likely to be a series of national and international regulations aimed at the digital economy. These will cover everything from ensuring content is safe and lawful, seeking to eradicate harmful disinformation or 'fake news' campaigns, and ensuring technology firms are appropriately taxed for their activities. The importance of protecting citizen data will remain high on the global agenda, and is likely to be even more so as third parties seek to use sensitive data such as patient health and care information to provide ever more personalized services.

It is likely that there will continue to be a bifurcation of the digital economy along geographic lines. China, highly likely to be the world's largest economy within the next digital era, has a digital infrastructure closely linked to the state that is almost unrecognizable to the rest of the world. Amazon, Google and Facebook have extremely limited market penetration. Instead, national companies such as Tencent, Alibaba and Baidu provide the bulk of the country's digital services. Political tensions may exacerbate these differences, leaving companies based outside of China struggling to operate through restricted firewalls.

Wearables, robotics and sensors will continue the rise of the IoT

The 'Internet of Things' (IoT) will continue to be normalized as wearables – such as Apple's iWatch – crop up across all manner of use cases. From robot social care assistants to building sensors designed to identify pre-emptive repair work, devices – enabled by improved connectivity through high-speed broadband and 5G networks – will build up an ever-expanding treasure trove of data that will allow companies to optimize and improve their operations. As more people get used to such devices, expect them to become socially acceptable and used in all manner of settings. In your digital transformation, make sure to consider where such devices might help meet your user needs and, critically, develop a plan for making best use of the abundance of data that this presents.

Machine learning to advance, but general artificial intelligence and quantum computing will flatter to deceive

The fanfare around general artificial intelligence, the quest to make computers act or behave as well as humans, or quantum computing, which affords the possibility of processing exponentially more data and calculations than ever before, somewhat detracts from some of the real and amazing developments achieved in the field of 'narrow' artificial intelligence. This latter category, mainly the mainstay of algorithms and machine learning techniques, has made use of data to optimize decision-making in fields as diverse as sports, probation and justice, health and care and education. As the cost of data storage continues to decrease and as companies seek to make machine learning approaches 'as-a-service' (in other words, possible without in-house machine learning specialists), it's likely that the barriers to successfully deploying ML in most organizations will drop. As this happens, you may wish to position yourself at the front of the queue to capitalize on its potential benefits. As discussed in Chapter 12, there are lots of good arguments for trying to do this sooner, but if you do, be prepared to pay a high price with uncertain returns.

An on-demand society

The American author William Gibson once famously declared that 'the future is here, it's just not very evenly distributed.' This quote can aptly describe a number of the considerations in this chapter. The 'on-demand' society has actually been a pretty quotidian experience in certain parts of the world for some time already. The ecommerce retail delivery platform Dada Group pioneered one-hour delivery windows across China in 2020, and many customers in major cities across the world have already come to expect grocery deliveries using platforms such as DoorDash, Deliveroo or Uber in similar timescales. It's unlikely that such 'on-demand' expectations will abate, particularly as digital on-demand streaming services for music, gaming, and film and television are now common currency. It will be vital to meet such elevated customer expectations. If you can't promise your customers 'on-demand' satisfaction, someone else probably will.

Ecommerce as default

One of the most pronounced shifts in consumer behaviour that was exacerbated by the Covid-19 global pandemic was buying patterns. Whereas only 7 per cent of all retail sales (excluding automotive fuel) were conducted online in 2010, by May 2020, a third of all retail sales were online.[3] While this will vary by industry, the long-run march of ecommerce as a preferred way of buying is unlikely to slow down. For businesses, this means ensuring at a bare minimum that they have a means of transacting with customers online – have logistics relationships in place, booking slots, online payment mechanisms and so forth. Smart digital leaders should go further, however, and fully interrogate where their business should sit in the end-to-end value chain from customer desire to customer receipt of a good or purchase. Should a business only be a small part of this value chain (for instance, by sending goods to a third-party retail platform) or would the business be better off looking to capture more of the value chain? All decisions here have trade-offs, but should be actively considered: the less you control of the value chain, the more dependent you are on others for fulfilling your customers' needs.

Remote working and continued near- and off-shoring

Covid-19 also forced many sectors – particularly professional services – to work remotely across the globe. It seems highly probable that at the very least a mixed economy of working patterns will emerge, with expectations for 'on-site' office presence diminishing. This is likely to be particularly the case for scarce technology talent. While there remain important reasons for teams to get together in person – if only to allow the more sociable and fun parts of working life to flourish – expect businesses to need to be more flexible in catering for remote working provision. This may present many great opportunities to your business, particularly when hiring tech talent. You should use this as a pretext to look beyond national boundaries when recruiting. However, you will also most likely need to invest in the technology available to facilitate hybrid working effectively. It's one thing having everyone Zoom into a meeting; it's a different technology requirement having some teams together in person with others joining virtually. You'll need to make sure a two-tier hierarchy doesn't emerge between 'in-person' and 'virtual' staff members.

Personalization of digital through biotechnology

The personalization of customer experiences has been a long-running trend in digital; your Facebook, Twitter, Amazon and sometimes even local authority council homepages will all be tailored to your interests and needs. The big data revolution, underpinned by the changes covered in Chapter 12, is now affecting the world of biotechnology. In this field the so-called 'omics revolution (covering genomics, transcriptomics, proteomics and metabolomics) promises to transform how health and care is delivered through tailoring medicines and treatments. Messenger RNA (mRNA) technology was critical in developing effective vaccines against coronaviruses in the early 2020s, and the subsequent venture capital investment in this field is likely to unleash new developments. Expect opportunities to emerge for companies that can capitalize and make use of the enormous scale of data involved in such areas.

Cybersecurity as the dominant security concern of the age

As we covered in Chapter 14, there are a lot of bad actors out there intent on hurting businesses and governments. Given the rapidly increasing volumes of data, devices and points of attack, expect cybersecurity to be the major security worry for leaders in this digital era. While you should do everything to ensure the basic building blocks of cyber defences are in place, you will also need to be continuously on your guard against new and emerging threats and have robust plans in place should an attack strike.

AR and VR will look to improve on IRL

Augmented and virtual reality technologies have been around for some time, but as of 2020 the price point for them remains high: a Microsoft HoloLens costs several thousand dollars. Expect these prices to drop as the hardware becomes cheaper to manufacture and more developers join its community, thus providing more potential revenue streams for the technology. These technologies will look to enhance, rather than replace, 'in replace life' (IRL) experiences and can be applied to diverse potential use cases from training to dating. Significant improvements in infrastructure such as 5G (broadband cellular networks) will enable high bandwidth technologies such as AR and VR to thrive.

Sustainability as the norm

As we discussed in Chapter 15, consumer expectations will drive many businesses to adopt aggressive decarbonization targets. Be prepared to review and, if necessary, radically change your supply chain to ensure you are doing your bit. The media, politicians and customers will look unkindly on organizations that are using dirty energy, and may come to expect clean energy sources – such as solar, wind, geothermal and so forth – to be used by default. If you cannot demonstrate your commitment to sustainability, do not be surprised to suffer a backlash.

Where next?

Whether you agree with the 12 predictions above – or whether they have been rendered obsolete with the passing of time – Figure 17.1 nonetheless presents a useful framework for thinking about the future. Gather a multidisciplinary group across your organization to run a 'future storm' session where you identify current and potential future issues that might affect your company in the decades ahead. Use the four quadrants of the framework as inspiration for the session. When it comes to the 'chance' bucket, think laterally – what are the potential big changes that could occur, and try to group them by type. Natural disaster, geopolitical, or other. It's important that you have a plan not for the specific but for the general here.

Once you have your horizon-scanned list of opportunities and threats, prioritize which of these you want to take action on first. You may, for instance, decide on commissioning some work on sustainability immediately, investigating options for using clean energy in your company, for instance, or decarbonizing pension investment pots. Keep this list regularly under review and look to conduct 'future storm' sessions at regular intervals so you are always thinking ahead.

BRINGING THE PRINCIPLE TO LIFE
The many horizons of Netflix

With an estimated market capitalization of $125 billion in 2020, Netflix is an undisputed giant of the technology world. It's story is an exemplary case study in the importance of constantly pursuing the next horizon of innovation. Netflix has gone through three transformations in its business model. Each transformation can be thought of as a horizon that it embraced, dominated and then moved on from.

Its first horizon, beginning from its corporate birth in 1997, was to own and disrupt the DVD rental market. With Blockbuster the dominant market leader, Netflix instead offered a direct-to-home rental order business model that offered a different level of convenience to its competitors. It then built on its early successes with a subscription model that captured customers and provided ongoing revenue streams.

Where it went next is perhaps most surprising. Despite having established a highly effective business model, Netflix tore up its own rulebook by moving on to a new horizon: direct-to-home streaming of film and television content. This risked cannibalizing its own market share and reducing revenues from its mail-order services. But, having spotted significant changes in consumer behaviour (many of which were brought about by music streaming sites such as Napster) and cognizant of the way improved internet speeds were allowing consumers to access more content and faster than ever before, Netflix seized the opportunity and never looked back.

However, not satisfied with creating two successful business models, by the 2010s Netflix sought to build a new horizon: content creation. Whereas Netflix had previously run a 'platform' style business model – effectively the broker between content creators and end consumers – it now sought to capture more of the value chain by moving into content creation. With the advent of major shows with then Hollywood stars such as *House of Cards*, Netflix moved into a new competitive arena, this time fighting against major production houses such as Disney and Fox. It seems likely a new horizon will emerge in the next digital era for one of the most innovative companies of the 21st century.

Tips and tricks

- Keep your predictions general in nature. The more precise they are, the more likely they are to be wrong.

- You don't need to have a plan to react to every eventuality, but you do need to have generalizable approaches for reacting to general trends.

- Investing in the future is risky and uncertain. Make sure your stakeholders know this – especially your finance colleagues.

- There are two ways of adapting to the changing world: leading the innovation or following the innovators. Either can work, but you can't afford to do nothing.

- Review your predictions periodically. If you're getting things right or wrong, is there something you can learn from this that can help to inform future predictions?

What you might say in your next meeting

Successful digital businesses don't stand still.

Netflix has built three successful business models – we're still struggling with one.

We don't exist in a vacuum. We need to be constantly adapting to the changing world around us.

Who's going to join me for a 'future storm' session?

What's on the next horizon for us?

Where you can find out more

Companies such as Gartner specialize in helping to make sense of future technology trends. It's worth reading up on their publications and familiarizing yourself with the Gartner 'Hype Cycle', which is a powerful way of understanding why some technologies fail and others succeed. Twitter is a particularly popular medium for keeping abreast of emerging innovations – try following well-regarded thinkers in this space such as Azeem Azhar and those in their circles.

Notes

1 Statista (2021) Search engine market share worldwide, March, www.statista. com/statistics/216573/worldwide-market-share-of-search-engines/ (archived at https://perma.cc/L4YN-RJV9); StatsCounter (2021) Social media stats worldwide, April, gs.statcounter.com/social-media-stats (archived at https:// perma.cc/3687-7DYM); Canalys (2021) Global cloud infrastructure market Q4 2020, 2 February, www.canalys.com/newsroom/global-cloud-market-q4–2020 (archived at https://perma.cc/TVF9-GTSB)

2 The product engineer Patrick Rivera has written some thought-provoking things about the future of cryptocurrency. You can find out more about his work by following him on Twitter @patrickxrivera

3 Eley, J (2020) A nation of shopkeepers shaken by the shift online, *Financial Times*, 15 August

Conclusion

10 principles for digital transformation

To conclude, these are the principles that should guide your thinking as you embark on your digital transformation journey.

Principle 1: Put *all* users at the heart of your thinking

User-centricity is transformational. It means placing the needs of real people first, beyond any technological or bureaucratic considerations. Your digital roadmap will be explicitly developed through real and thoughtful engagement with your users. By being user-centred, you will delight those that interact and engage with your products and services. You will remove waste from your organization by deprioritizing things that don't add value to users. And you will be agile and responsive as user demands change over time.

An important nuance to user-centricity is that *customers are not your only users*. A progressive digital organization will make brilliant digital services for all of its critical user groups. This will undoubtedly include end-users – usually customers – but also may include internal users, regulators and even suppliers. This means designing digital products and services that make life better for administrators, developers, intermediaries and more. You do not get diminishing returns from user-centricity. The more user-centred you are for all, the better.

Principle 2: Set a vision and iterate towards it

A digital vision sets out a series of objectives and outcomes. It will be informed by a combination of deep user research, market and competitor analysis, and underlying business needs. The vision will be time-bound and should put markers in the sand – stage-gates – at which points you should evaluate progress. If your digital vision is too prescriptive, it risks failing before it even has standards. The field of digital, data and technology is constantly and rapidly changing. You need to make a virtue of its dynamism.

The best way to deal with this rapidly changing landscape is through iteration and experimentation. Agile approaches can help. But more than anything, you need to rid yourself of rigid expectations. Focus on outcomes more than the minutiae of deliverables. If you do the latter, you immediately risk breaching our first principle, because you are assuming you know what users think and want from the outset. You cannot know this in advance. So welcome the uncertainty, keep your eyes fixed on achieving your end goals, and enjoy the ride.

Principle 3: Embrace agile ways of working

Agile ways of working will make your digital transformation efforts nimbler, cheaper and focused on meeting user needs. Agile teams, practices and culture are different from traditional ways of working. Whereas the previous orthodoxy of waterfall approaches prize certainty and specificity in plans many years ahead, agile accepts that much of the world is complex, unknowable and unpredictable.

To contend with these challenges, agile approaches place a primacy on minimal viable product (MVP) development. For any technology project – be it an end-user device rollout or a machine learning algorithm – MVP thinking means you should start small, test continuously with users, iterate as necessary and only scale up if and when ready. In doing so, you will kill a lot of ideas and stop a lot of projects. But remember: it's much better to stop something that's never going to work sooner rather than later.

Principle 4: Fund with failure in mind

Paying for digital isn't simple. Inflated user expectations, unrealizable promises from suppliers and working cultures resistant to change can all lead to failure, or at least perceived failure. When this happens, those picking up the bill for the digital transformation will usually vow never to make the same mistakes again and, as a consequence, turn to either the cheapest or biggest technology supplier in the future in the false expectation that this will somehow protect them from future failures.

The reality of doing anything new and different is that the very nature of change means it won't always work. Even rolling out established technologies can bring unexpected hiccups. As such, when you're preparing budgets for digital transformation, make sure three safeguards are in place. First, don't overpromise on the potential benefits from your work. While this may help to get a business case through in the short term, in the longer term you'll live to regret the unrealistic expectations hanging over you. Second, always apply optimism bias to your forecast costs. This will give you a buffer if things go awry. And third, try and break down the work into chunks. This should allow you to call it a day at various points if necessary. When you do, make sure you learn lessons from what did and didn't work.

Principle 5: Get the right skills and talent in place

Just as you wouldn't ask a gas engineer to paint your house, you shouldn't ask an IT project manager to code software. Yet many digital transformation efforts go wrong through simple category errors: by assuming that all 'digital' jobs are alike and that by cobbling together a rainbow of random digital professionals you can make some magic happen. Instead, you need to carefully work out, based on your digital roadmap, what skills you need, from whom and when.

Doing so should present big challenges to your established business model. Should you use consultants, contractors or hire permanent team members? If they're consultants, how do you make sure you get the best value from them and don't become reliant on them in the future? If you choose contractors, who's going to help you manage them? And if you're going down the permanent hire route – which, even if money were no object, may be hard due to the scarcity of supply – then a multitude of questions arise. Which part of your organization will these staff sit in? Who do they report to? How will you evaluate their work? What will be their career progression route, and so forth? But don't be put off by these big considerations – it's essential you confront them head on. Without the right people, you'll never make change happen.

Principle 6: Focus relentlessly on the data

In its most simple description, digital transformation is about using data to improve the lives and experiences of people. Everything in the digital world – hardware, software, sensors, transistors – ultimately boils down to sending, manipulating and receiving data. This data is encoded as binary digits – 0 and 1 – and from this everything follows.

As such, you need to constantly have in the forefront of your mind questions about the nature of the data your systems use, create and interoperate with. How do you know that your organization's data is of high quality and integrity? How can you best use the data to improve the operations of your organization? Where is your data stored and is it protected? Who has access to your data and do you have consent of the individuals from whom the data is derived? What regulations and laws do you need to comply with? All your technology stack considerations should be based around answering these questions. Without good data, you can't achieve anything.

Principle 7: Expect to be attacked

Just like an office anywhere in the world will have physical security measures in place, every organization should also have digital security measures in place. The rapidly increasing volume of cyber attacks since the 2000s means it is a question of when, not if, your organization will experience some form of attack. You may already be under attack but you just don't know it yet.

Your cyber defences need to plan for multiple scenarios. You need to know what to do to protect yourself against such scenarios, but also what to do if you are the victim of an attack. While much should be done to protect your technology infrastructure, don't lose sight of the fact that the weakest link in your organization is almost certainly your employees and how they interact with your organizational infrastructure. Train them in cybersecurity best practice. Remind them. Audit their practices. Remind them again, and so forth.

Principle 8: Always do the right thing

Your transformation should be ethical by default. At minimum you need to comply with all regulations and laws. This should seem blindingly obvious, yet the history of technology is littered with firms who have failed to meet this most basic expectation. Beyond this, you need to remember that you are undertaking a digital transformation for the future, not the past. And as such, your ethical considerations need to be for the world as you wish it to be, not as it has been.

Eradicating bias from your processes, fostering a diverse and inclusive workforce, breaking down gender barriers, helping tackle the climate crisis, contributing to local communities – this is a non-exhaustive list of issues you need to be proactively addressing. Remember that in a globalized, platform-based world, you will undoubtedly rely on a wide range of suppliers. It's vital to keep an eye on your suppliers to ensure that they too share your values and ethics.

Principle 9: Make your positive contribution to the digital world

The modern internet era was founded on principles of openness, transparency and sharing. It would be fair to say that the current digital era does not quite represent the desired aspirations of the early internet innovators. Closed developer systems, fake news and disinformation, and mass data capture of citizens all fly in the face of what the internet was supposed to be. In the words of Tim Berners-Lee, inventor of the World Wide Web, in 2006: 'Freedom of connection, with any application, to any party, is the fundamental social basis of the Internet.'[1] We have diverged some distance from this vision.

While you don't necessarily need to only adopt open-source technologies (though there may be much merit in this), you should make sure you are making a positive contribution to the digital world. This means sharing code, insights and learnings openly. It means being open and transparent with your customers about how you use their data. And it means building and facilitating connections between different systems and networks outside of your organization, to the end benefit of users.

Principle 10: Look to the next horizon

We nearly got through a book on technology without mentioning Moore's Law: the observation that the number of transistors that can fit on a silicon chip can double at least every two years. While Moore's observation is neither a law nor entirely accurate anymore, it speaks to a wider truth: the pace of change in the digital world is frighteningly quick. This matters especially because your customers will engage in technology in all parts of their life, and so a significantly improved experience in one field is likely to lead to heightened expectations in another. In short, you can't stand still. You need to always be working hard to improve things for users.

This can be a challenge to many organizations. It might mean cannibalizing existing customers or shutting down profitable services because you're building something *even better*. It will mean constantly staying abreast of new trends – curious but not naive about their potential. As daunting as this may seem, it should also be exciting. The digital world is full of possibilities to make things better. And these possibilities should always be open to you.

Note

1 Berners-Lee, T (2006) Net neutrality, *Scientific American*

APPENDIX

A framework for understanding digital, data and technology

A simplified guide to how it all fits together.

Anatomy of a digital, data and technology ecosystem

Know your software development kits (SDKs) from your APIs? What's the difference between client-side and server-side? Where would you implement robotic process automation (RPA)? While this book has tried – as far as possible – to not get too stuck in the weeds of technology acronyms and nomenclature, it's an indisputable fact that digital transformation operates its own quirky, often confusing, language.

With this in mind, Figure A.1 presents a simplified articulation of a digital ecosystem. A generic health and care example is given, but really, with a bit of imagination, you should be able to translate this into retail, aviation, education or any other sector. The purpose of this is to give you a little bit of extra orientation for where things fit together when you hear various buzzwords. A quasi-glossary then follows, explaining the various terms.

FIGURE A.1   A simplified digital ecosystem

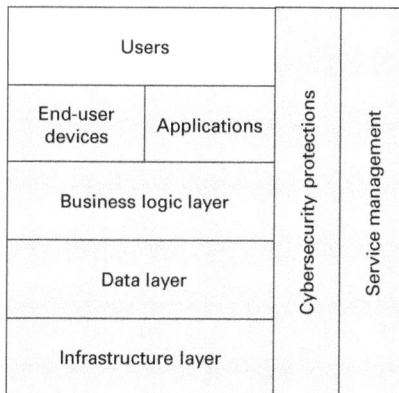

Users

In our simplified health and care ecosystem, you would expect users and their rough user needs to include:

- *Patients:* 'I want to get better.'
- *Clinicians:* 'I want technology to help me do my job better.'
- *Regulators:* 'I need to know if the system is working properly.'
- *Administrator:* 'I want technology to help me in my day-to-day work.'

There will be many more users and user needs, but these should capture the majority of technology considerations.

End-user devices

This will cover a panoply of hardware and physical devices. For patients, this could include: wearable devices like pulse oximeters for self-care; blood sugar trackers for diabetes care; robotic prosthesis to aid movement; or even sensors to detect motion at home to enable independent living. For clinicians, user devices might include so-called 'computers on wheels' that follow clinicians as they do day-to-day ward rounds, or tablets to capture clinical notes, or digital dictation tools. Administrators may have their own devices – barcode scanning tools for instance – to track goods throughout a hospital.

Applications

This is a broad term to cover the large swathes of software that users interact with. Applications exist on your phones (which will work on either an Android or iOS operating system) or can be web applications, which can be accessed through the internet. Applications will use front-end coding technologies such as HTML, CSS and JavaScript to 'abstract' data and information from a wider technology stack and present it to you, as the user, in a friendly and intuitive format. This is often known as a graphical user interface (GUI). These applications should also be able to receive and transmit data from the user.

From a user perspective, in our health and care example, applications could include everything from patient portals that allow users to access and view their health and care data, to data analysis and visualization applications (such as PowerBI or Tableau). The latter might be used by administrators or regulators to understand how effectively a service is running, for instance. The application side is sometimes referred to as the 'client side', because it is where the client (the 'user') interfaces with the technology.

Business logic layer

Here data from applications is manipulated so that it can be stored, processed or analysed. Coding languages such as Ruby, Python, Java or PHP will be used to interact with the databases in the data layer. There may be an overlap between applications and business logic if you are looking to apply machine learning techniques. In these instances, data is likely to be extracted or accessed from underlying data layers which then interface with a data scientist who trains algorithms to try and answer specific questions. In our health and care example, an administrator may wish to understand if certain patient groups can be risk-profiled for specific diseases. A data scientist would extract, cleanse and then train algorithms to see if such a question could be answered – the outputs would then be shared with the administrator.

Much application development also occurs in the business logic layer. This is where application programming interfaces (APIs) are used in earnest: code is written to expose certain parts of business logic for other developers to access. An API call could be used, for instance, to share patient data safely and securely between different applications and programs. Software development kits (SDKs) are also used frequently in this layer. SDKs are programming kits made available by specific hardware or operating systems. So, for instance, Apple, Microsoft, Kubernetes (an open-source operating system) all release SDKs that are available to developers for programming. For developers wishing to make applications on an iPhone to track a user's heart rate, for instance, they would need to use the iOS SDK.

Data layer

Often known as the 'server side', this is where data is stored and where data can be extracted in order to serve the business logic layer. It's incredibly important that good standards are maintained to ensure data quality and integrity. In the health and care world, Fast Healthcare Interoperability Resources (FHIR) standards are set to guide how data should be maintained and shared to facilitate ease of sharing information between different data systems. This is particularly important in health and care where a large number of different electronic patient record systems act as repositories for patient information. In order to provide a joined-up care experience so that while you might be under the care of a doctor in one city a clinician in another can still view your information, standards such as FHIR are invaluable.

Techniques such as robotic process automation (RPA) – the automation of routine tasks – are popular in this layer. These can help save human time; where an individual may have to physically clean data before analysis, RPA techniques could potentially replace this human element.

Infrastructure layer

This covers everything from physical services to cloud servers and core hardware such as routers which enable internet connectivity. Server storage will typically consist of a choice from the main cloud computing providers (AWS, Azure, Google) or in-house servers on premises. If the latter approach is taken, servers will need to be secured and stored in the requisite ambient room temperatures. While this has historically been seen as the domain of 'IT people', it's important that digital approaches are still adopted here. For example, a user-centred approach can fundamentally change how an infra-structure layer is generated. Your decision about router placement or bandwidth provider should be informed by your end-user requirements.

Emerging technologies such as blockchain – effectively decentralized server networks – may also be used in this layer as alternative providers of data storage and access. The application of blockchain technologies is also relevant to other layers. Smart contracts, for instance, which provide encrypted agreements between parties, will be both user-facing and reach down into blockchain infrastructure layers.

Cybersecurity protection

This should run across all layers. Penetration testing and vulnerability awareness exercises should run across the technology layers. Encryption should run throughout: from the https pages used in web applications through to the scrambling and anonymization of patient data. Staff and end-user training is critical, as is access control (ensuring only those that should have access do have access) to end-user devices. In a health and care setting, patient information is hugely sensitive. A stolen, unlocked iPad that has access to a patient's notes would be an awful breach of patient confidentiality. Even worse, a stolen, unlocked iPad that has unprotected access to a whole database of patient information would be a disaster.

Service management

What happens if the machine to track a patient's vital signs stops working? Or if a server goes down that provides access to patient records? This is where you need service management to step in. Service management can include call centres, helpdesks, as well as IT engineers who can be deployed on site to fix a problem. Unless you are in the business of creating all of your technology stack (which no one is), you will be reliant on the services of others; for these services, make sure you have contractual arrangements in place for supporting when something goes wrong and you need help.

INDEX

Italics denote figures and tables.